TARLA DALAL

India's #1 Cookery Author

100% Vegetarian

S&C

SANJAY & CO.

MUMBAI

Third Printing : 2001

Copyright @ Sanjay & Co.
ISBN No. 81-86469-45-1

Price Rs. 230/-

PUBLISHED & DISTRIBUTED BY
SANJAY & COMPANY
353 A-1, Shah & Nahar Industrial Estate, Dhanraj Mill Compound,
Lower Parel (W), Mumbai - 400 013. INDIA
Tel (91-22) 496 8068 Fax : (91-22) 496 5876 Email : sanjay@tarladalal.com
Website : www.tarladalal.com

Research Team
Pinky Dixit
Aarti Kamat
Jyoti Jain

Printed by
Jupitar Prints, Mumbai

Designed by
Satyamangal Rege

Food Stylist
Nitin Tandon

Photography
Vinay Mahidhar

Illustrations
Ganesh Tayde

Other Books by Tarla Dalal

INDIAN COOKING

Tava Cooking

Rotis & Subzis

Desi Khana

The Complete Gujarati Cook Book

Mithai

Achaar aur Parathe *New*

The Rajasthani Cookbook *New*

GENERAL COOKING

Exciting Vegetarian Cooking

Party Cooking

Microwave Cooking

Quick & Easy Vegetarian Cooking

Saatvik Khana

Mixer Cook Book

The Pleasures of Vegetarian Cooking

The Delights of Vegetarian Cooking

The Joys of Vegetarian Cooking

Cooking With Kids

Snacks under 10 minutes

WESTERN COOKING

The Complete Italian Cook Book

The Chocolate Cook Book

Eggless Desserts

Mocktails & Snacks

Soups & Salads

Mexican Cooking

Easy Gourmet Cooking

TOTAL HEALTH

Low Calorie Healthy Cooking

Pregnancy Cookbook *New*

Baby and Toddler Cookbook *New*

MINI SERIES

A New World Of Idlis & Dosas

Cooking Under 10 Minutes

Pizzas And Pasta

Fun Food For Children

Roz Ka Khana

Microwave-Desi Khana

T.V. Meals *New*

INTRODUCTION

Chaat... every Indian is familiar with this word and has tasted chaat in some form or the other! And everyone has tangy tasty memories of the street or locality where they have eaten the most delectable panipuri or pav bhaji.

The vast and mysterious sub-continent of India has a range of cuisines as diverse as its cultures which includes an amazing array of street foods. Eating on the streets is a way of life for our people. Street vendors hawk a variety of freshly cooked food to hungry passers-by at all times of the day and the mouth-watering sight and smell of crispy hot samosas, flaky khasta kachoris, hot and syrupy gulab jamuns surrounds you at all times.

Food cooked on the streets has necessarily to be prepared quickly and with so many hawkers vying for passing trade, the appearance, aromas and flavours of the food are of paramount importance.

This book is a carefully prepared combination of classic and traditional favourites. Most of the chaat recipes are adapted to cater to modern trends in healthy eating. Among the classics, you will find all the famous recipes ranging from the simple ones like bhelpuri, pav-bhaji, dabeli to the more elaborate hariyali tikkis and potato baskets. There is also a whole lot of innovative recipes which are simply irresistible and lip smacking like the Samosa Kadhi Chaat.

Also included is a section of home-made slushes and sorbets and of course the famous streetside accompaniments like malpuas, gulab jamuns, jalebis which are a must have before, with or after a fiery round of chaats.

Whether you want a family meal, a snack or an easy to prepare but impressive dish to serve to friends, you will find plenty to choose from here.

Step into the kitchen with this book and you will realise how easy it is to create these tongue tickling recipes for yourself!!

Tarla Dalal

CHAATS

SWADISHT RAASTE KE CHAAT

MANPASAND CHAAT

PAUSHTIK CHAAT

CHAAT KE SAATH

CHAAT KE BAAD KUCH MITHA

CHATPATI CHUTNEYS

BASIC RECIPES

Swadhist Raaste Ke

CHAAT

BHEL PURI

This is the most commonly sold chaat in the streets of Mumbai. Almost every street has its own friendly bhelwala with his inimitable blends of chutneys and masalas.
Bhel is a delectable combination of papadis, puffed rice, sev, onions, potatoes, raw mango and chutneys.
The proportions of the various chutneys can be changed to adjust to your personal preferences. Toast the puffed rice to make it crisp before using it to make bhel. If you store the puffed rice, sev and papadi and refrigerate or freeze the chutneys, you can rustle up a heavy snack in a jiffy for your hungry kids returning from school.

Preparation time : 10 minutes.   No cooking.   Serves 4.

4 cups puffed rice (mamra)
1 cup nylon sev or sev, page 113
20 papadis, page 110
½ cup chopped onions
½ cup boiled potatoes, chopped
2 teaspoons fresh garlic chutney,
page 106
8 tablespoons khajur imli ki chutney, page 102
4 tablespoons green chutney, page 105
1 teaspoon black salt (sanchal)
juice of ½ lemon
salt to taste

For the garnish
8 papadis, page 110, crushed
1 tablespoon finely chopped
raw mango (optional)
4 tablespoons nylon sev or sev,
page 113
2 tablespoons chopped coriander

1. Combine all the ingredients in a large bowl and toss gently till all the ingredients are well mixed.
2. Divide into 4 equal portions and garnish each portion with the papadis, raw mango, sev and coriander.
   Serve immediately.

Handy tip : Nylon sev is a very thin variety of deep fried besan sev used as a topping for chaats. It is readily available at most provision stores.

SEV PURI

*This is another favourite chaat sold on Mumbai streets.
Every bhelwala has his own recipe of sev puri.
Sev puri, as the name indicates is sev topped on puris or papadis, along with
potatoes and chutneys. Tangy, crisp and tongue tickling are some words that come to
my mind when I think of sev puri.
The very thought makes my mouth water as I reach out to make this
delicious chaat!*

Preparation time : 10 minutes   **No cooking**   **Serves 4.**

24 papadis, page 110
½ cup boiled potatoes, chopped
½ cup onions, finely chopped
2 tablespoons finely chopped raw mango
2 teaspoons fresh garlic chutney, page 106
8 tablespoons khajur imli ki chutney, page 102
4 tablespoons green chutney, page 105
1 teaspoon chaat masala, page 111
juice of ½ lemon
salt to taste

For the garnish
½ cup nylon sev or sev, page 113
2 tablespoons chopped
coriander

1. Arrange the papadis on a serving plate.
2. Top each papadi with a little potato, onion and raw mango.
3. Top the papadis with some fresh garlic chutney, khajur imli ki chutney and green chutney.
3. Sprinkle with chaat masala, lemon juice and salt on top.
4. Garnish with the sev and coriander.
   Serve immediately.

DAHI BHEL

Bhel literally means a "mixture". Dahi Bhel is another mixture recipe - a mixture of papadis and pineapple, along with the goodness of beans, curds and of course a melange of chutneys. Tasty, crunchy and chatpata!

Preparation time : 20 minutes.　　　**No cooking.**　　　**Serves 3 to 4.**

15 to 20 papadis, page 110, crushed
1 tablespoon chopped pineapple (optional)
1 potato, boiled and cubed
1 tablespoon finely chopped raw mango
4 tablespoons white chick peas (kabuli chana) or green peas, boiled
2 to 3 tablespoons meethi soonth, page 107
1½ to 2 tablespoons green chutney, page 105
½ cup fresh curds, whisked
2 teaspoons cumin seed (jeera) powder
2 teaspoons chilli powder
2 teaspoons chaat masala, page 111
salt to taste

1. Mix the crushed papadis, pineapple, potato, raw mango, chick peas, meethi soonth, green chutney and curds in a bowl.
2. Sprinkle the cumin seed powder, chilli powder and chaat masala on top. Serve immediately.

PAPADI CHAAT

What we commonly know as sev puri in Mumbai is known as Papadi chaat in Delhi.
It is similar, but not the same. Papadi chaat as the name suggets has lots of papadis,
tossed in a blend of chutneys, curds and potatoes.
Mix the papadis, chutneys and curds the way you want.

Preparation time : 15 minutes.   No Cooking.   Serves 6 to 8.

1 recipe papadis, page 110
1 recipe khajur imli ki chutney, page 102
1 recipe green chutney, page 105
2 medium potatoes, boiled and sliced
2 cups fresh curds, whisked
1 teaspoon chaat masala, page 111
1 teapsoon cumin seed (jeera) powder
1 teaspoon chilli powder
salt to taste

1. Combine the papadis, khajur imli ki chutney, green chutney and salt in a large serving bowl and mix well.
2. Top with the potatoes and whisked curds.
3. Sprinkle chaat masala, cumin seed powder and chilli powder on top. Serve immediately.

PANI PURI

Picture on page 26

Crisp semolina puris filled with sprouts and chilled mint flavoured water make a great snack for a hot summer afternoon. They are known as "Golgappas" in North India and as "Poochkas" in West Bengal.
When my favourite "panipuriwallah" is serving me these delightful little puris one after the other,
I just go on eating till I can eat no more!
Sprouts can be replaced with hot ragda, page 35, to complement the chilled mint water. Making the puris takes some time to master and although they can be bought from a local store. The extra effort put in to make them at home is well worth the trouble. Do remember to store the puris in an air-tight container. You can always refresh them by baking them in a slow oven for 4 to 5 minutes.

Preparation time : 25 minutes.   Cooking time : 25 minutes.   Serves 4.

For the puris
½ cup fine semolina (rawa)
½ tablespoon plain flour (maida)
2 to 3 tablespoons soda water (bottled)
salt to taste
oil for deep frying

For the pani
1½ cups chopped mint leaves
1 tablespoon chopped coriander
⅓ cup tamarind (imli)
25 mm. (1") piece ginger
4 to 5 green chillies
1 teaspoon roasted cumin seed (jeera) powder
1½ teaspoons black salt (sanchal)
salt to taste

Other ingredients
1 recipe khajur imli ki chutney, page 102
½ cup mixed sprouts, boiled, page 114
½ cup boondi, page 115, soaked and drained

For the puris

1. Combine the semolina, plain flour, soda water and salt to make a semi-stiff dough and knead well. Allow it to rest under a wet muslin cloth for 10 to 15 minutes.
2. Divide the dough into 40 equal portions and roll each portion in 37 mm. (1½") circles.
3. Place these circles under a damp cloth for about 5 minutes.

14

4. Deep fry in a kadhai in hot oil on a medium flame till they puff up and are golden brown (Press each puri using a slotted spoon till they puff up in the oil).
5. Remove, drain on absorbent paper and store in an air-tight container.

For the pani

1. Soak the tamarind in ½ cup of water for approximately 1 hour. Strain out all the pulp through a sieve.
2. Combine this pulp with the remaining ingredients except the black salt in a blender and grind to a fine paste using a little water.
3. Transfer the paste into a large bowl and combine with 1 litre of water, the black salt and salt and mix well.
   Chill for at least 2 to 3 hours after making so that all the flavours have blended properly.

How to proceed

1. Crack a small hole in the centre of each puri.
2. Fill with a little sprouts or boondi, then top a little khajur imli ki chutney, immerse it in the chilled pani and eat immediately.

Handy tip : You can use ragda, page 35, instead of the sprouts or boondi.

DAHI PURI

After a round of spicy pani puris, eating dahi puris is the perfect way to soothe your palate."Dahi puris" are a favourite with children as well as with adults who cannot handle the fiery pani puri.

What makes a dahi puri truly divine is obviously the humble curds which are made daily in every Indian household. The curds have to be fresh and chilled and most importantly of the right consistency i.e. neither too thick or too thin.

If your curds are not very fresh, add a few tablespoons of milk to cut down the sharp acidic taste. Save the semi-puffed (half puffed) or damaged puris which cannot be used for serving pani puri to make dahi puri.

Preparation time : 25 minutes.   No Cooking.   Serves 4.

1 recipe puris, page 14
⅔ cup mixed sprouts, page 114
⅔ cup boiled potato, cubed
1 cup khajur imli ki chutney, page 102
3 cups fresh curds, whisked
salt to taste

For the garnish
½ cup nylon sev or sev, page 113
2 teaspoons chilli powder
2 teaspoons roasted cumin seed (jeera) powder
2 tablespoons chopped coriander

1. Arrange the puris on a serving plate.
2. Crack a small hole in the centre of each puri.
3. Add salt to the curds and mix well.
4. Fill it with the mixed sprouts, potato, khajur imli ki chutney and top with fresh curds.
5. Sprinkle the nylon sev, chilli powder and cumin seed powder on top.
6. Garnish with the chopped coriander and serve immediately.

MUSHROOM KATHI ROLL

*Satisfying hungry children is a task in itself. Every day food has to look interesting and of course different to please their appetites! This recipe is of a delicious chapati roll filled with a spicy mushroom mixture. The addition of soda bi-carb to the chapati dough makes these chapatis soft while
the cornflour makes them crispy.
A treat for children and adults alike! If you're using left-over chapatis to rustle up a tasty snack, just warm them up a little!*

Preparation time : 20 minutes.   Cooking time : 15 minutes. Makes 4 rolls.

For the rotis
1 cup plain flour (maida)
½ tablespoon cornflour
¼ teaspoon soda bi-carb
½ tablespoon butter
salt to taste

For the mushroom bhurji
2 cups mushrooms, finely chopped
3 cloves garlic, finely chopped
1 teaspoon grated ginger
1 large onion, finely chopped
2 tomatoes, finely chopped
2 teaspoons coriander-cumin seed (dhania-jeera) powder
2 teaspoons pav bhaji masala
3 teaspoons dried fenugreek leaves (kasuri methi)
¼ cup tomato purée
2 tablespoons cream
a pinch of sugar
¼ cup chopped coriander
1 tablespoon oil
salt to taste

Other ingredients
ghee for cooking

For the rotis
1. Sieve the flour, cornflour, soda bi-carb and salt.
2. Rub in the butter and make a soft dough using as much water as required.
3. Knead very well, cover with a wet muslin cloth and keep aside for ½ hour.
4. Knead once again and divide into 4 portions.
5. Roll each portion as thinly as possible. Cook lightly on a tava (griddle) on both sides using a little ghee and keep aside.

For the mushroom bhurji

1. Heat the oil in a pan, add the garlic, ginger and onion. Sauté till the onion turns translucent. Add the tomatoes and cook till the oil separates.
2. Add the coriander-cumin seed powder, pav bhaji masala and kasuri methi.
3. Mix well, add the tomato purée and cook for a few more minutes.
4. Add the mushrooms and salt and stir well till the mushrooms are cooked.
5. Add the cream, sugar and coriander and mix well. Keep aside.

How to proceed

1. Divide the filling into 4 portions.
2. Spread a portion of the filling evenly on each roti and roll it like a Swiss roll.
3. When you want to serve, cook the rolls on a tava with ghee until crisp.
4. Cut into 50 mm. (2") pieces and serve hot.

KATHI ROLLS

"Kathi Rolls" as they are known in North India are hot crispy rotis served with a choice of fillings. This mouth-watering recipe originated as a good way to use up left-over chapatis which were warmed in ghee or butter and rolled up with a spicy vegetable mixture with a sprinkling of chaat masala.

These rolls are versatile enough to be served at any time of the day and can even land up at a party as a cocktail snack! Use any combination of vegetables you like e.g. paneer, corn or green peas to make these vegetarian Indian "Frankies".

Preparation time : 30 minutes. Cooking time : 15 minutes. Makes 8 rolls.

For the rotis	To be mixed into a filling
2 cups plain flour (maida)	4 boiled and mashed potatoes
1 tablespoon cornflour	2 tablespoons chopped coriander
½ teaspoon soda bi-carb	1 onion, chopped
1 tablespoon butter	1 green chilli, chopped
salt to taste	1 teaspoon chaat masala, page 111
	1 tablespoon lemon juice
Other ingredients	salt to taste
ghee for cooking	

For the rotis
1. Sieve the flour, cornflour, soda bi-carb and salt.
2. Rub in the butter and make a dough by adding enough water.
3. Knead very well, cover with wet muslin cloth and keep aside for ½ hour.
4. Knead once again and divide into 8 portions.
5. Roll each portion as thinly as possible. Cook lightly on a tava on both sides using a little ghee and keep aside.

How to proceed
1. Divide the filling into 8 portions.
2. Spread one portion of the filling evenly on each roti and roll it like a Swiss roll.
3. When you want to serve, cook the rolls on a tava with ghee until crisp.
4. Cut into 50 mm. (2") pieces and serve hot.

CHOLE BHATURE

My earliest memories of Chole Bhature is of the one I ate at a popular eatery in Mumbai known as "Cream Centre". On enquiring, I was told that the chick peas and spices were simmered together for hours resulting in a dish that a large number of Mumbaites relish even today!

My version of chole is however, ready in minutes and is as delicious. I have also added tea leaves, which impart a dark brown colour to the chick peas which usually comes from simmering chick peas in an iron pot.

I enjoy eating hot chole with tikkis, bhaturas, khulcha or simply topped on a slice of bread. Crisp, yet spongy bhaturas are used to mop up the chole. Traditionally bhatura dough was made using leavening agents like soda, curds and leaving it for hours to ferment before they could be rolled out and deep fried.

This recipe of bhatura is one that uses mashed potatoes to soften up the bhaturas. Moreover, also these bhaturas do not turn rubbery and chewy when they are eaten cold.

Preparation time : 45 minutes.   Cooking time : 1 hour.   Serves 4.

For the chole, Pic. on page 103
1 cup chick peas (Kabuli chana), soaked overnight
1 tea bag or 1 teaspoon tea leaves, tied in a muslin cloth (optional)
½ teaspoon cumin seeds (jeera)
1 onion, finely chopped
12 mm. (½") piece ginger, grated
2 cloves garlic, grated
2 teaspoons chole masala (chana masala)
2 teaspoons chilli powder
2 teaspoons amchur (dry mango powder)
¼ teaspoon turmeric powder (haldi)
1 tablespoon coriander (dhania) powder
1 teaspoon cumin seed (jeera) powder
2 tablespoons oil
salt to taste

For the bhature
½ cup plain flour (maida)
½ cup potato, boiled and grated
1½ teaspoons oil
salt to taste
oil for deep frying

For serving
1 onion, sliced
4 lemon wedges

For the chole
1. Pressure cook the chick peas with the tea bag for 3 whistles until they are soft. Drain and keep aside. Discard the tea bag.
2. Heat the oil in a pan and add the cumin seeds. When the seeds crackle, add the onion, ginger and garlic and sauté till the onion is golden brown.
3. Add the chole masala, chilli powder, amchur, turmeric powder, coriander powder, cumin seed powder and salt and sauté for another minute.
4. Add the chick peas and 1 cup of water and mix well. Simmer for 10 to 15 minutes. Keep aside.

For the bhature
1. Combine the flour, potato, 1½ teaspoons of oil and salt and knead into a firm dough without using any water.
2. Knead the dough very well till it is smooth.
3. Cover with a wet muslin cloth and rest the dough for 10 minutes.
4. Divide the dough into 4 equal parts and roll out into circles of 125 mm. (5") diameter.
5. Deep fry in hot oil till the bhaturas puff up and both sides are golden brown. Serve hot with the chole, sliced onion and lemon wedges.

Handy tips :
1. *While frying the bhature, press the centre lightly with a frying spoon so as to help it to puff up.*
2. *Chole masala is a blend of spices which is readily available at most grocery stores.*

VADA PAV

Mumbai's very own burger. The vada is made of a spicy potato filling deep fried in a gram flour batter. Along with a hot and spicy garlic chutney, it is served inside small square breads locally known as "laddi pav". I have fond memories of sharing a vada pav with my son while travelling on a business trip to Vapi by train. Although vada pav is a Maharashtrian dish, I was surprised to find it popular even in Gujarat. Another travelling ritual on my frequent drives to Pune is to stop at a small café on the highway to grab a quick vada pav and a steaming hot cup of masala tea that chases away all my travel fatigue.

Preparation time : 10 minutes. Cooking time : 30 minutes. Makes 8 pieces.

8 laddi pavs (small squares of white bread)
1 recipe dry garlic chutney, page 106

For the vada filling
1½ cups boiled and mashed potatoes
2 green chillies, chopped
1 tablespoon ginger, grated
1½ tablespoons garlic, grated
1 teaspoon mustard seeds (rai)
¼ teaspoon asafoetida (hing)
6 to 8 curry leaves
½ teaspoon turmeric powder (haldi)
1 tablespoon oil
salt to taste

For the outer covering
¾ cup Bengal gram flour (besan)
¼ teaspoon turmeric powder (haldi)
a pinch soda bi-carb
1 teaspoon oil
salt to taste

Other ingredients
oil for deep frying

For the vada filling
1. Pound the green chillies, ginger and garlic using a mortar and pestle.
2. Heat the oil and add the mustard seeds. When they crackle, add the asafoetida curry leaves and sauté for a few seconds .
3. Add the pounded mixture and sauté again for a few seconds.
4. Add the potatoes, turmeric powder and salt and mix well.
5. Remove from the fire and cool.
6. Divide into 8 equal portions. Shape into rounds.

For the outer covering
1. Combine all the ingredients in a bowl and make a batter using approximately ⅓ cup of water.
2. Dip each round of the vada filling into the batter and allow it to coat the mixture well.
3. Deep fry in hot oil till golden brown. Drain on absorbent paper and keep aside.

How to proceed
1. Slice each pav into half and spread some dry garlic chutney inside.
2. Place one vada in each pav and serve immediately.

Note :
Laddi pavs are small square shaped white bread rolls which are available at local bakeries. You can also use bread rolls or slices if the pav is not available.

DABELI

Picture on facing page

This is traditionally sold on the streets of Gujarati towns. It is another version of vada pav made with a sweet and spicy potato mixture which is filled into a small burger bun and then topped with onion, pomegranate, fresh garlic chutney and sev.
Instead of pomegranate, you can use black or green grapes cut into small pieces.

Preparation time : 10 minutes. Cooking time : 15 minutes. Makes 15 buns.

For the dabeli masala
1 red chilli
1 teaspoon coriander (dhania) seeds
½" (12 mm.) stick cinnamon
2 cloves
¼ teaspoon cumin seeds (jeera)

For the filling
1 cup boiled and mashed potato
½ teaspoon cumin seeds (jeera)
a pinch asafoetida (hing)
2 teaspoons dabeli masala, receipe above
2 tablespoons khajur imli ki chutney, page 102
2 tablespoons oil
salt to taste

Other ingredients
15 small burger buns
butter or oil for cooking

To serve
1 onion, chopped
½ cup roasted peanuts
½ cup chopped coriander
½ cup nylon sev or sev, page 113
½ cup fresh pomegranate(anar)
2 teaspoons fresh garlic chutney, page 106
6 tablespoons khajur imli ki chutney, page 102

1. **Pav,** *page 28*
2. **Pav Bhaji,** *page 28*
3. **Chaat Masala**, *page 111*
4. **Dabeli** *recipe above*

For the dabeli masala
1. Roast all the ingredients in a pan for 2 to 3 minutes.
2. Grind to a fine powder in a blender. Use as required.

For the filling
1. Heat the oil in a pan and add the cumin seeds. When they crackle, add the asafoetida, dabeli masala, potato, salt and ½ cup of water and mix well.
2. Remove from the fire, add the 2 tablespoons of khajur imli ki chutney and mix well. Divide into 15 portions. Keep aside.

How to proceed
1. Slice the burger buns into halves horizontally and cook the buns in a pan using a little butter.
2. Place a portion of the filling on the lower half of each bun.
3. Top with the chopped onion, peanuts, coriander, sev, pomegranate , fresh garlic chutney and khajur imli ki chutney.
4. Sandwich it with the top halves of the burger buns.
   Serve hot.

1. **Limca Phudina Pani,** *page 37*
2. **Puris,** *page 14*
3. **Kewra Pani,** *page 37*
4. **Boondi,** *page 115*
5. **Khajur Imli Pani,** *page 37*
6. **Mixed Sprouts,** *page 114*

PAV BHAJI

Picture on page 25

A hurried meal for the man in the street. This is a spicy blend of vegetables in tomato gravy served with pav that is cooked with butter. This is truly an innovation that arose out of the necessity of providing a nice hot meal in a hurry and one that tickles the taste buds.

When I am lazy to cook on an entire meal for my family, pav bhaji in one of the first few dishes which comes to mind. It is easy to cook and also filling.
Round it off with a slice of kulfi or a scoop of ice-cream.

Preparation time : 15 minutes.   **Cooking time : 20 minutes.**   **Serves 4.**

For the pav
8 laddi pavs
(small squares of white bread)
4 tablespoons butter
1 teaspoon pav bhaji masala
(optional)

To be ground into a chilli-garlic paste
3 to 4 Kashmiri chillies, soaked in warm water
4 to 6 cloves garlic

For the bhaji
1½ cups potatoes, boiled and mashed
1 cup cauliflower, finely chopped
½ cup green peas
½ cup carrots, chopped
1 cup onion, chopped
½ cup capsicum, finely chopped
2½ cups tomatoes, chopped
½ teaspoon turmeric powder (haldi)
½ teaspoon chilli powder
1½ tablespoons pav bhaji masala
½ teaspoon black salt (sanchal)
4 tablespoons butter
salt to taste

For serving
1 large onion, chopped
4 lemon wedges
1 tablespoon chopped coriander

For the bhaji
1. Boil the cauliflower, peas and carrots till they are soft. Drain out the excess water.
2. Heat the butter in a large pan, add the onion and capsicum and sauté for 2 minutes. Then, add the prepared chilli-garlic paste and sauté till the onion softens.
3. Add the tomatoes and simmer till the oil separates.
4. Add the turmeric powder, chilli powder, pav bhaji masala, black salt and salt and cook for 2 to 3 minutes.
5. Add the boiled vegetables and potatoes and mash thoroughly using a potato masher, adding ½ cup of water if required.

For the pav
1. Slice each pav into 2 horizontally. Apply a little butter to each side and sprinkle with a little pav bhaji masala, if desired.
2. Heat a large tava and cook the pav on both sides till the pieces are lightly browned.

How to proceed
1. Serve the hot bhaji on 4 individual plates and top with the onion and coriander.
2. Serve with the hot pav and lemon wedges.

Handy tip : Pav bhaji masala is a spice blend which is readily available at most grocery stores.

MASALA PAV

Masala pav is a spicy blend of tomato onion gravy cooked and stuffed inside butter laden pavs. Every pav bhaji vendor serves his own version of Masala Pav so that each one tastes different but equally delicious.
Very often the pav bhaji gravy is tossed with pieces of pav and served with a slice of lemon. It is a spicy way to serve bread. Quick and easy!

Preparation time : 5 minutes.   Cooking time : 20 minutes.   Makes 4 pavs.

4 laddi pavs (small squares of white bread)
2 tablespoons butter

For the masala
1 large onion, chopped
½ capsicum, chopped
2 cloves garlic, finely chopped
2 tomatoes, chopped
½ teaspoon turmeric powder (haldi)
½ teaspoon chilli powder
½ teaspoon black salt (sanchal)
½ teaspoon pav bhaji masala
2 tablespoons butter
salt to taste

For the garnish
2 tablespoons chopped coriander
lemon wedges

For the masala
1. Heat the butter in a pan and sauté the onion and capsicum till the onion is translucent.
2. Add the garlic, tomatoes, turmeric powder and chilli powder and sauté for a further 5 minutes.
3. Add the black salt, pav bhaji masala, and salt and mix well.
4. Keep aside.

How to proceed
1. Slice each pav into half horizontally. Heat the butter on a tava (griddle) and grill the pav on both sides till crisp.
2. Add the cooked masala and coat the pav in it.
3. Serve hot, garnished with the coriander and lemon wedges.

KHASTA KACHORI

"Khasta" actually means "flaky" and this flaky kachori is filled with a delectable moong dal mixture and deep fried. Remember to fry the kachori on a very slow flame so that the crust is crisp and gets cooked on the inside.
A perfect kachori is one that is puffed up and flaky outside but hollow inside. This dish can be stored in air-tight containers for upto a week. When unexpected guests arrive, warm up the kachoris in a slow oven for about 7 to 10 minutes, fill them with curds and chutneys and serve.

Preparation time : 15 minutes. Cooking time : 45 minutes. Makes 12 kachoris.

For the dough
2 cups plain flour (maida)
½ teaspoon salt
¼ cup melted ghee or vanaspati

For the filling
½ cup yellow moong dal (split yellow gram), soaked for 4 hours
1 teaspoon cumin seeds (jeera)
¼ teaspoon asafoetida (hing)
1 teaspoon green chilli-ginger paste
1 teaspoon chilli powder
1 teaspoon garam masala
1 tablespoon amchur (dry mango powder)
2 tablespoons Bengal gram flour (besan)
3 tablespoons oil
salt to taste

Other ingredients
oil for deep frying

For serving
2 cups beaten curds
green chutney, page 105
khajur imli ki chutney, page 102
chilli powder
roasted cumin seed
(jeera) powder
chopped coriander
nylon sev or sev, page 113

For the dough
1. Combine all the ingredients and knead into a firm dough using a little water. Knead very well for 5 to 7 minutes.
2. Divide the dough into 12 equal parts and keep covered under a wet muslin cloth.

For the filling
1. Heat the oil in a pan and add the cumin seeds and asafoetida.
2. When the seeds crackle, add the soaked and drained moong dal and sauté for a few seconds.
3. Add the green chilli-ginger paste, chilli powder, garam masala, amchur, gram flour and salt and stir for 5 to 7 minutes till the masalas are cooked.
4. Cool and divide into 12 equal portions. Shape each portion into a ball and keep aside.

How to proceed
1. Roll out each portion of the dough into a circle of 50 mm. (2") diameter.
2. Place one portion of the filling mixture in the centre of the rolled dough circle.
3. Surround the filling mixture with the dough by slowly stretching it over the filling mixture.
4. Seal the ends tightly by pinching them together and remove any excess dough, if necessary.
5. Roll each filled portion into a circle of 62 mm. (2½") diameter taking care to ensure that the filling does not spill out.
6. Gently press the centre of the kachori with your thumb.
7. Deep fry over low heat in hot oil till golden brown on both sides. The kachoris should puff up like puris. These take a long time to fry as the crust is thick and need to be cooked on the inside also.
8. Cool and keep aside.

To serve
1. Place one kachori on a serving plate and make a hole in the centre.
2. Fill it with 3 to 4 tablespoons of the beaten curds.
3. Top with green chutney, khajur imli ki chutney, chilli powder, cumin seed powder, salt and coriander.
4. Sprinkle sev on top and serve immediately.

Handy tip : The kachoris can also be eaten without the curd topping. Just serve them with kajur imli ki chutney, page 102.

VARIATION : MINI KHASTA KACHORIS Picture on page 77
You can make 24 small kachoris using the above recipe.

DAHI VADAS

This recipe is popular all over India. Different communities have their own variations to this recipe. For example, some add sugar to the curds, whilst others temper it with mustard and curry leaves. The Marwaris use moong dal instead of urad dal to make the vadas.

Dahi vadas can be eaten as a snack or as part of the meal.
The vadas can be made a day in advance and refrigerated. You have only to soak them in hot water and drain just before serving.

Preparation time : 20 minutes. Cooking time : 15 minutes. Makes 12 dahi vadas.

For the vadas
½ cup urad dal (split black lentils), soaked for 4 hours
12 mm. (½") piece ginger
2 green chillies
a pinch soda bi-carb
salt to taste

For the garnish
chilli powder
roasted cumin seed (jeera) powder

For serving
3 cups beaten curds
2 tablespoons kajur imli ki chutney, page 102
salt to taste

For the vadas
1. Wash and drain the urad dal.
2. Grind together the urad dal, ginger, green chillies and salt in a food processor to a coarse paste.
3. Add the soda bi-carb to the urad dal paste and mix well till the batter is light and fluffy. Add a little water if required.
4. Wet your hands and take 2 tablespoons of the batter on your palm or on a sheet of wet plastic and shape into a circle of 25 mm. (1") diameter. Deep fry in hot oil on a slow flame till the vadas are golden brown for about 10 minutes. Drain on absorbent paper.

How to proceed
1. Soak the deep fried vadas in water for about 45 minutes.
2. Just before serving, drain and squeeze out the excess water.

3. Arrange the vadas on a serving dish and top with beaten curds.
4. Garnish with chilli powder, cumin seed powder and salt and serve with khajur imli ki chutney.

ALOO AUR SHAKARKAND KI CHAAT

Most of us consider sweet potatoes to be a very boring vegetable, only to be eaten during religious fasts and then too, it is only baked or boiled before it is peeled and eaten.
This recipe is a good example of how versatile and delicious the humble potato and sweet potato can be.
If you omit the radish in this recipe, you can also eat this dish when "fasting".

Preparation time : 10 minutes. Cooking time : 20 minutes. Serves 4.

2 large potatoes
2 medium sweet potatoes (shakarkand)
4 tablespoons green chutney, page 105
½ cup khajur imli ki chutney, page 102
1 cup fresh curds, beaten
¼ teaspoon black salt (sanchal)
½ teaspoon roasted cumin seed (jeera) powder
¼ teaspoon chilli powder
½ cup grated white radish (mooli)
4 tablespoons oil
salt to taste

1. Boil the potatoes and sweet potatoes in salted water. Peel and cut into large cubes.
2. Heat the oil in a not-stick pan and sauté the potato and sweet potato cubes till they are golden brown.
3. Drain on absorbent paper and place in a serving dish.
4. Top the cubes with the green chutney, khajur imli ki chutney, curds, black salt, cumin seed powder, chilli powder and salt.
5. Garnish with the grated radish.
   Serve hot.

RAGDA PATTIES

This dish actually makes a complete meal and one that takes very little cooking, especially if you have planned ahead and soaked the peas a day before. You can use a filling of your choice for the patties like peas, french beans, paneer, corn etc.
I also like to eat just the ragda topped with the onion and chutneys with pav instead of the patties.

Preparation time : 15 minutes.   **Cooking time : 90 minutes.**   **Serves 6.**

For the ragda filling
1 cup dried yellow peas (white vatana)
2 boiled potatoes, cut into small pieces
¼ teaspoon turmeric (haldi) powder
½ teaspoon chilli powder
2 teaspoons green chilli-ginger paste
½ teaspoon garam masala
2 teaspoons jaggery (gur), grated
1 tablespoon tamarind (imli), soaked
salt to taste

For the tempering (for the ragda)
¼ teaspoon mustard seeds (rai)
6 curry leaves
a pinch asafoetida (hing)
2 tablespoons oil

For the patties
1 kg. potatoes
2 tablespoons cornflour
salt to taste

To be ground into a mixture for the filling (for the patties)
1 cup chopped mint leaves
¼ cup chopped coriander
4 green chillies
12 mm. (½") piece ginger
juice of ½ lemon
1 teaspoon sugar
salt to taste

Other ingredients
oil for deep frying

To serve
1 recipe green chutney, page 105
½ recipe fresh garlic chutney, page 106
½ recipe khajur imli ki chutney, page 102
1 cup nylon sev or sev, page 113
1 cup onions, chopped

For the ragda

1. Soak the dried peas overnight.
2. Drain, add approximately 3 to 4 cups of fresh water and pressure cook for 4 whistles or until the peas are soft.
3. Prepare the tempering by heating the oil, adding the mustard seeds, curry leaves and asafoetida and stirring till the mustard seeds crackle.
4. Add in all the other ingredients for the ragda adding more water if required. Mix wel, mashing the peas slightly so that the gravy becomes thicker.
5. Simmer for 10 minutes and keep aside.

For the patties

1. Boil, peel and grate the potatoes.
2. Add the cornflour and salt and knead to a soft dough.
3. Divide into 12 equal portions and keep aside.
4. Roll out each portion into a 75 mm. (3") diameter circle. Place a portion of the ground filling mixture on each circle.
5. Bring together the edges in the centre to seal the filling inside the potato.
6. Press lightly on top to make a patty.
7. Repeat to make the remaining 11 patties.
8. Shallow fry on a non-stick pan till the patties are golden brown and crisp.

How to proceed

1. For serving, place 2 patties on a plate and pour the ragda over.
2. Top with all the chutneys. Sprinkle the sev and onions on top. Serve immediately.

Handy tip : For crisper patties, use old potatoes or a variety commonly called "chips" or "wafer potatoes". You might need to add some more cornflour to the potatoes if they are not dry enough.

PANI PURI DELIGHT

Picture on page 26

This is a delightful journey for your palate. It is truly a fantasy for anyone who is a pani puri addict like me. I enjoyed this unforgettable journey on the streets of Delhi where we began with the hing pani, which was sharp, and then proceeded to a mellowed down jeera pani followed with sweet date and tamarind flavoured water. We moved on to a lemony mint water and finished with a dessert-like kewda flavoured water.

It does take a lot of time and effort to make these flavoured waters but I assure you they will be well worth it.

All these can be made upto a day in advance and refrigerated.

Preparation time : 4 hours.   **No cooking.**   **Serves 4 to 6.**

For the hing pani
2 tablespoons tamarind (imli)
1 tablespoon coriander (dhania) powder
¼ teaspoon asafoetida (hing)
¼ teaspoon chilli powder
¼ teaspoon black salt (sanchal)
½ teaspoon chaat masala, page 111
salt to taste

For the kewra pani
Picture on page 26
¼ cup sugar
½ teaspoon black salt (sanchal)
½ teaspoon chaat masala, page 111
juice of ½ lemon
2 to 3 drops kewra essence

For the Limca phudina pani
Picture on page 26
1 bottle Limca (lemon) drink
1 cup mint leaves
2 to 3 green chillies
½ teaspoon black salt (sanchal)
½ teaspoon chaat masala, page 111
½ teaspoon roasted cumin seed (jeera) powder
salt to taste

For the khajur imli pani
Picture on page 26
½ recipe khajur imli ki chutney, page 102, mixed with 2 cups of water

1 recipe puris, page 14
1 cup boondi, page 115, soaked and drained

For the hing pani
1. Combine all the ingredients with 2 cups of water in a large bowl.
2. Allow it to rest for 3 to 4 hours.
3. Strain through a muslin cloth and add 1 more cup of water. Mix well.
4. Chill before serving.

For the jeera pani
1. Substitute the asafoetida in the recipe for hing pani with 1 tablespoon of cumin seeds (jeera), roasted and tied in a muslin cloth. Chill before serving.
2. Remove the cumin tied in muslin cloth just before serving.

For the Limca phudina pani
1. Grind the mint leaves and chillies to a paste in a blender.
2. Combine with the remaining ingredients and 1½ cups of water.
3. Chill for at least 3 to 4 hours before serving.

For the kewra pani
1. Combine the sugar with 2½ cups of water and cook till the sugar has dissolved completely.
2. Allow to cool completely. Add the black salt, chaat masala, lemon juice and kewra essence and mix well.
3. Chill for 2 to 3 hours before serving.

How to proceed
1. Make a hole in the centre of each puri.
2. Fill each puri with a little boondi.
3. Serve one filled puri dipped in the hing pani, the second puri dipped in the jeera pani, the third puri dipped in the khajur imli pani, the fourth puri dipped in the Limca phudina pani and the fifth dipped in the kewra pani.
4. Repeat for the remaining puris.
   Serve immediately.

Handy tips :
1. The puris are eaten in the above mentioned order.
2. The Limca phudina pani can even be served as a delicious jaljeera.

Manpasand

CHaat

KATORI CHAAT

Picture on page 51

Mini tarts filled with a spicy mixture of sprouts and chutneys.
I have suggested baking the tart cases but you can stack them up and deep fry them in oil. The cases can be made days in advance and keep well when stored in an air-tight container.
Just rustle up the filling and serve these pretty tarts to display your culinary skills to your family and friends.

Preparation time : 15 minutes. Cooking time : 40 minutes. Makes 12 pieces.

For the katoris
½ cup plain flour (maida)
¼ cup butter, softened
¼ teaspoon salt

For the filling
1 cup mixed sprouts, page 114, boiled
½ teaspoon cumin seeds (jeera)
a pinch asafoetida (hing)
2 teaspoons chilli powder
2 teaspoons coriander-cumin seed(dhania-jeera) powder
¼ teaspoon turmeric (haldi) powder
1 teaspoon amchur (dry mango powder)
1 teaspoon chole masala (chana masala)
2 tablespoons oil
salt to taste

For serving
beaten curds
khajur imli ki chutney, page 102
green chutney, page 105
nylon sev or sev, page 113
chaat masala, page 111

For the katoris

1. Combine the flour, butter and salt and make a stiff dough using a little water. Knead very well.
2. Divide the dough into 2 equal portions.
3. Roll out each dough portion into a sheet of 6 mm. (¼") thickness.
4. Cut rounds of pastry using a large 50 mm. (2") diameter cookie cutter and press into tart moulds.

5. Prick all over with a fork.
6. Bake in a hot oven at 230°C (450°F) for 10 to 15 minutes.
7. Cool the tart cases.

For the filling
1. Heat the oil in a pan and add the cumin seeds. When they crackle, add the asafoetida.
2. Add the sprouts, chilli powder, coriander-cumin seed powder, turmeric powder, amchur, chole masala, salt and 2 tablespoons of water and mix well. Cook on a slow flame for 4 to 5 minutes. Keep aside.

How to proceed
1. Fill each tart with a portion of the filling.
2. Top with curds, khajur imli ki chutney, green chutney, sev and chaat masala. Serve immediately.

Handy tip : Chole masala is a spice blend that is easily available at provision stores.

KANJI VADAS

"Kanji" is a liquid extract of a food - usually rice, black carrots or mustard. This is a Marwari delicacy of moong dal wadas, soaked in mustard flavoured kanji. The kanji has to be made at least a day in advance so that all the flavours are released into the water. Mustard kanji is usually enjoyed in the winter, as mustard is a food which produces heat in the body.
Serve plenty of kanji with the vada so that one can enjoy a large sip of the kanji once the vada is polished off.

Preparation time : 1 day.   Cooking time : 15 minutes.   Serves 4.

For the kanji
¼ cup split mustard seeds (rai ka kuria)
1 tablespoon black salt (sanchal)
1½ teaspoons chilli powder
salt to taste

Other ingredients
oil for deep frying

For the vadas
2½ cups yellow moong dal (split yellow gram), soaked for 4 hours
1 teaspoon green chilli-ginger paste
½ teaspoon fennel seeds (saunf)
¼ teaspoon asafoetida (hing)
salt to taste

For the kanji
1. Combine all the ingredients and grind to a fine powder.
2. Dissolve this powder in 1½ litres of water, cover and keep refrigerated for 24 hours to allow all the flavours to blend.

For the vadas
1. Drain and grind the moong dal to a coarse paste using very little water.
2. Add the green chilli-ginger paste, fennel seeds, asafoetida and salt and mix well.
3. Wet your hands, take 2 tablespoons of the dal paste on your palm or on a sheet of wet plastic and shape into a circle of 25 mm. (1") diameter. Repeat with the remaining paste.
4. Deep fry in hot oil till golden brown in colour.
5. Drain on absorbent paper and cool.

42

How to proceed

1. Soak the vadas in water for 1 hour. Drain and squeeze out all the water by pressing each vada gently between your palms.
2. Place the vadas in the kanji and allow them to soak for at least 1 hour. Serve chilled.

Note : In cold weather, you need not refrigerate the kanji once it is made.

PALAK PAKODA CHAAT

Large spinach leaves, coated with a thin gram flour batter, are deep fried to make crisp spinach pakodas which are topped with sweet chutney and sprinkled with roasted cumin powder.
Here are all the ingredients of a delicious chaat!

Preparation time : 10 minutes. Cooking time : 15 minutes. Serves 6.

50 fresh spinach leaves, washed	**For serving**
1 cup Bengal gram flour (besan)	6 tablespoons meethi soonth, Page 107
½ teaspoon chilli powder	1 teaspoon roasted cumin seed
salt to taste	(jeera) powder
oil for deep frying	¼ teaspoon chilli powder

1. Mix the gram flour, chilli powder and salt with ¾ cup of water to make a thick batter.
2. Heat the oil in a kadhai and when hot, dip each spinach leaf in the gram flour batter and drop a few leaves at a time into the hot oil. Fry until golden brown, remove and drain on absorbent paper. Repeat for the remaining spinach leaves.
3. Place the spinach pakodas on a serving plate. Spread with the meethi soonth and sprinkle the cumin powder and chilli powder on top. Serve immediately.

PANEER TIKKI AUR CHOLE

Tikki chole is one of the more popular chaats in North India.
One afternoon when I was left with the task of feeding my hungry grandchildren, I
thought of making the most of what was available on my kitchen shelf. I then chanced
upon this recipe which has today become very popular
amongst my family and friends.
It took some time to master the art of making crisp alu tikkis. I use old potatoes
(which are commonly referred to as wafer potatoes) to make the tikkis crisp and a
slice of soaked bread to not only bind the potatoes but also to make them more
crunchy. The paneer filling for tikkis uses tomato purée which adds
a sharp tangy taste to it.
If you are one of those who would like to avoid deep frying the tikkis (all of us think it
a crime to eat deep fried food), you can shallow fry them
on a griddle (tava) using a little oil.
Chole along with these tikkis makes it a heavy snack. But you will enjoy the tikkis by
themselves with a little green chutney.

Preparation time : 15 minutes. Cooking time : 30 minutes.   Serves 3 to 4.

For the tikkis
1½ cups boiled potatoes, grated
3 tablespoons cornflour
1 bread slice (with the crust removed)
salt to taste

Other ingredients
bread crumbs for coating
oil for deep frying

For the filling
½ cup paneer (cottage cheese), crumbled
½ teaspoon cumin seeds (jeera)
¼ teaspoon turmeric powder (haldi)
1 teaspoon chilli powder
2 teaspoons coriander (dhania) powder
2 tablespoons tomato purée
1 medium onion, chopped
2 tablespoons chopped coriander
1 tablespoon oil
salt to taste

For serving
1 recipe chole, page 20
4 lemon wedges
1 onion, chopped

44

For the tikkis

1. Soak the bread in water. Squeeze out the excess water and crumble it.
2. Mix the potatoes, cornflour, crumbled bread and salt and knead well into a soft dough.
3. Divide the mixture into 10 equal portions, shape into even sized rounds and keep aside.

For the filling

1. Heat the oil in a pan and add the cumin seeds. When they crackle, add the turmeric powder, chilli powder, coriander powder, tomato purée and salt and sauté for 1 minute.
2. Add the paneer and mix well. Cook for one minute more.
3. Remove from the fire, add the onion and coriander and mix well.
4. Divide the mixture into 10 equal portions.

How to proceed

1. Flatten out each potato portion into a 50 mm. (2") diameter circle. Place a portion of the filling in the centre of each circle.
2. Bring together the edges in the centre to seal the filling inside the potato. Repeat with the remaining portions to make 9 more tikkis.
3. Roll the filled potato tikkis in bread crumbs and flatten them slightly.
4. Deep fry in hot oil till golden brown.
   Serve hot with the chole, lemon wedges and chopped onion.

Handy tips :
1. *Use old potatoes (wafer potatoes) to get crisper tikkis.*
2. *You will need 3 to 4 medium sized boiled potatoes for 1½ cups of grated potatoes.*

DAHIWALE ALOO KI SUBZI AUR URAD DAL PURI

Picture on page 52

This is a streetside snack from Central India. "Puri Bhaji" was everyone's favourite dish for breakfast, especially in the olden days, when everyone lived in joint families and puris were considered the quickest to make.
This recipe of puris uses an urad dal paste that gives bulk to the puris and also makes them crisper. Onion seeds add a hint of flavour to these puris. The aloo ki subji is a simple and delightful dish.

Preparation time : 30 minutes.   Cooking time : 30 minutes.   Serves 4.

For the dahiwale aloo
2½ cups peeled baby potatoes
½ teaspoon cumin seeds (jeera)
½ teaspoon mustard seeds (rai)
½ teaspoon onion seeds (kalonji)
½ teaspoon fennel seeds (saunf)
¼ teaspoon asafoetida (hing)
2 bay leaves
3 cloves
2 sticks cinnamon
3 to 4 curry leaves
1 green chilli, slit
2 teaspoons chilli powder
1½ teaspoons coriander-cumin seed
(dhania-jeera) powder
¼ teaspoon turmeric powder (haldi)
1 cup curds, beaten
2 tablespoons ghee
salt to taste

For the garnish
2 to 3 tablespoons chopped coriander

For the urad dal puris
½ cup urad dal (split black lentils)
1 teaspoon onion seeds (kalonji)
¼ teaspoon asafoetida (hing)
1 cup whole wheat flour (gehun ka atta)
1 teaspoon oil
salt to taste

oil for deep frying

For the dahiwale aloo
1. Heat the ghee in a pan and add the cumin seeds, mustard seeds, onion seeds, fennel seeds and asafoetida. When the seeds crackle, add the bay leaves, cloves, cinnamon, curry leaves and green chilli and sauté for a few seconds.
2. Add the potatoes, chilli powder, coriander-cumin seed powder, turmeric powder and salt and sauté till the masala coats the potatoes evenly.
3. Add ½ cup of water and bring to a boil.
4. Add the curds and bring to a boil while stirring continuously so that the gravy does not split.
   Garnish with the coriander.

For the urad dal puris
1. Clean, wash and soak the urad dal for 2 to 3 hours. Drain completely.
2. Purée the dal in a mixer using ¼ cup of water to make a fine paste.
3. Combine with the onion seeds, asafoetida, wheat flour and salt and knead into a soft dough.
4. Add the oil and knead again.
5. Cover the dough with a wet muslin cloth and allow to rest for 10 minutes.
6. Divide the dough into 12 equal portions and roll out each portion into a circle of 75 mm. (3") diameter.
7. Deep fry in hot oil over a medium flame till the puris puff up and both sides are golden brown. Drain on absorbent paper.
   Serve hot with the dahiwale aloo ki subzi.

KAND KI CHAAT

For all those who must be wondering what "kand" must be, it is actually a part of the yam family. It is also called "purple yam" and is available abundantly during the winter.
I actually bought some to make "Oondhiya" for my family, but since there was much more than I needed, I just deep fried cubes of kand and tossed the pieces in some fresh mint leaves and poppy seeds. What I had was a really tasty chaat recipe which I would like to share with everybody.

Preparation time : 10 minutes.   Cooking time : 25 minutes. Serves 4.

3 cups kand (purple yam), cut into 12 mm. (½") cubes
½ teaspoon cumin seeds (jeera)
¼ teaspoon asafoetida (hing)
1 large onion, chopped
2 to 3 green chillies, finely chopped
2 teaspoons poppy seeds (khus khus)
2 teaspoons amchur (dry mango powder)
1 tablespoon coriander (dhania) powder
1 teaspoon black salt (sanchal)
¼ cup chopped mint
¼ cup chopped coriander
1 tablespoon oil
salt to taste

Other ingredients
oil for deep frying
lemon wedges to serve

1. Deep fry the cubed kand in hot oil over a medium flame till cooked and crispy. Drain on absorbent paper and keep aside.
2. Heat 1 tablespoon of oil in another pan and add the cumin seeds and asafoetida. When the cumin seeds crackle, add the onion and green chillies and sauté for 2 to 3 minutes.
3. Add the poppy seeds and sauté for 1 to 2 minutes.
4. Add the deep fried kand, amchur, coriander powder, black salt, mint, coriander and salt and stir over a medium flame for 4 to 5 minutes. Serve hot with lemon wedges.

DAL PAKWAN

An extremely popular Sunday breakfast delicacy in Sindhi homes.
Chana dal served with crispy pakwans. The dal is thick, creamy and spicy. The
pakwans, though the name sounds intimidating, use the same papadi dough rolled
out into large chapatis and deep fried until crisp.
In order to obtain crispy unpuffed pakvans, always prick them
with a fork before frying.
It is also important to remember to fry them over medium heat
so that they are crisp.

Preparation time : 20 minutes.   Cooking time : 40 minutes.   Serves 6 to 8.

For the dal
225 grams split Bengal gram (chana dal)
2 medium onions, peeled and finely chopped
1 teaspoon cumin seeds (jeera)
2 green chillies, slit
½ teaspoon turmeric powder (haldi)
1 large tomato, finely chopped
2 tablespoons chopped coriander
1 teaspoon coriander-cumin seed
(dhania-jeera) powder
½ teaspoon chilli powder
¼ teaspoon garam masala
2 tablespoons ghee or oil
salt to taste

For the pakwans
2 cups plain flour (maida)
1 cup whole wheat flour (gehun ka atta)
1 teaspoon cumin seeds (jeera)
½ teaspoon salt
oil for deep frying

For serving
chopped onions
meethi soonth, page 107

For the dal

1. Clean, wash and soak the Bengal gram for 3 to 4 hours. Drain and keep aside.
2. Heat the ghee in a saucepan and fry the onions, cumin seeds and chillies until the onions are light brown in colour. Add the Bengal gram and turmeric powder. Season with salt and add ½ cup of water. Cover and cook on a slow heat for 15 to 20 minutes until the dal is soft.

3. Add the tomato, coriander, coriander-cumin seed powder and chilli powder and cook for 1 minute. Sprinkle the garam masala on top.

For the pakwans

1. Mix the flours, cumin seeds and salt with enough water to make a stiff dough. Knead well. Divide the dough into 15 portions. Roll out each portion into rounds of 125 mm. (5") diameter. Prick all over with a fork.
2. Heat the oil in a kadhai and when hot, add the pakwans one at a time. Deep fry until golden brown over medium heat till they are crisp and golden brown. Remove with a slotted spoon and drain on absorbent paper. Repeat for the remaining pakwans.

How to proceed
Serve the hot dal with the pakwans, onions and meethi soonth.

1. **Fresh Garlic Chutney,** *page 106*
2. **Katori Chaat,** *page 40*
3. **Pocket Chaat,** *page 63*
4. **Cheese & Broccoli Tikkis,** *page 63*

MOONG AUR MOOLI KI CHAAT

I have experimented with a lot of recipes for moong dal pakodis and this is probably the best I have come across. The addition of a little Eno's fruit salt makes the pakodis spongy and more crunchy and also makes them cook faster.
These moong dal pakodis must be eaten hot with fresh chilled curds and of course with the spicy green and sweet khajur chutney without which any chaat is incomplete. The use of grated mooli or white radish instead of sev is a refreshing change and reduces the calorie count.

Preparation time : 10 minutes. Cooking time : 20 minutes. Serves 4 to 6.

1 cup yellow moong dal (split yellow gram)
1 teaspoon chopped coriander
2 green chillies, finely chopped
1 onion, chopped
1 teaspoon ginger, grated
½ teaspoon Eno's fruit salt
salt to taste
oil for deep frying

For the tempering
1 teaspoon cumin seeds (jeera)
2 pinches asafoetida (hing)
1 tablespoon oil

For the topping
1 cup grated white radish (mooli)
¼ cup green chutney, page 105
2 tablespoons khajur imli ki chutney, page 102
1½ cups fresh curds, beaten
½ teaspoon chilli powder
1 teaspoon roasted cumin seed (jeera) powder
½ teaspoon black salt (sanchal)
1 teaspoon chaat masala, page 111

1. **Urad Dal Puris,** *page 46*
2. **Dahiwale Aloo ki Subzi,** *page 46*

1. Clean, wash and soak the moong dal for 4 hours. Drain out all the water.
2. Grind the moong dal to a paste without using any water.
3. Add the coriander, green chillies, onion, ginger and salt and mix well. Keep aside.
4. Make the tempering by heating the oil in a small pan and then adding the cumin seeds and asafoetida to it. When the cumin seeds crackle, pour the tempering over the prepared moong dal mixture. Mix well.
5. Sprinkle the fruit salt over the mixture and mix gently.
6. Fry spoonfuls of the mixture in hot oil (you will get approx. 25 pakodis).
7. Reduce the flame and deep fry till the moong pakodis are golden brown in colour.
8. Drain on absorbent paper and keep aside.

How to proceed
1. Place the hot moong pakodis on a serving plate.
2. Top with the radish, green chutney, khajur imli ki chutney, curds, chilli powder, cumin seed powder, black salt and chaat masala and serve immediately.

Handy tip : *Do not add the fruit salt to the mixture till the oil is hot and you are ready to fry the moong dal pakodis.*

POTATO BASKET CHAAT

Picture on page 77

These dainty potato baskets are made with potato straw and filled with a crunchy mixture of stir-fried bean sprouts and capsicum.
Selecting the right kind of potatoes is the most vital step in making these baskets. Use a variety of potato that is used to make wafers. Some vendors even call them "old potatoes". This variety of potato has more starch which results in crisper baskets and these potatoes do not even brown quickly. Old tea strainers which are made of metal can be used to make these baskets.
You can make these baskets a day or so in advance and store them in an air-tight container.

Preparation time : 15 minutes.   Cooking time : 40 minutes. Makes 10 baskets.

For the potato baskets
2 cups thickly grated potatoes (old potatoes)
oil for deep frying

For the filling
2 cups bean sprouts
½ cup red or yellow capsicum, finely chopped
¼ teaspoon pepper powder .
½ teaspoon chilli powder
¼ teaspoon dried ginger powder (soonth)
¼ teaspoon sugar
1 teaspoon amchur (dried mango powder)
½ teaspoon roasted cumin seed (jeera) powder
2 tablespoons chopped coriander
1 teaspoon butter
salt to taste

Other ingredients
½ cup green chutney, page 105

For the potato baskets
1. Soak the grated potatoes in cold water for 10 to 15 minutes.
2. Drain and wash in running water for about 5 to 7 minutes.
3. Drain and wipe dry using a dry absorbent cloth.

4. Divide the grated potatoes into 10 equal portions.
5. Place each portion of the grated potatoes on a 37 mm. (1½") diameter metal tea strainer and top with a second strainer as shown in the diagram below.

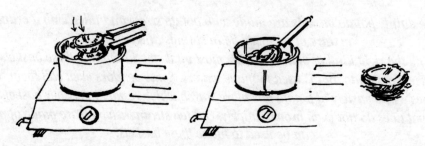

6. Hold firmly and deep fry in oil over a medium flame till the basket is golden brown. Remove the strainer from the oil, invert it and tap lightly to unmould the basket.
7. Repeat steps 5 and 6 to make 9 more baskets. Store in an air-tight container.

For the filling

1. Heat the butter and add the pepper powder, chilli powder, ginger powder and sugar and sauté for a few seconds.
2. Add the bean sprouts, capsicum, amchur, cumin seed powder, coriander and salt and cook for about a minute. Keep aside.

How to proceed

1. Put 3 to 4 tablespoons of the filling into each potato basket.
2. Top with a spoonful of the green chutney.
3. Arrange on a serving plate and serve immediately.

Handy tip : Old potatoes or chip / wafer potatoes are required to make crisp potato baskets. It is wise to invest in half a dozen metal strainers, once you are comfortable with the recipe so that the frying gets done quicker.

Picture on page 104

Traditionally, samosas are served with chutney or chole, but this one which is a personal favourite of mine, is a bit different. I have experimented serving them with a coconut kadhi and to add some crunch to the dish, I have added chopped spring onions. This chaat is a meal in itself!

The coconut kadhi uses coconut milk which is the liquid extracted with water from the coconut flesh. Coconut milk is now available in tetrapacks at grocery stores, so you need not go through the effort of extracting it!

Preparation time : 40 minutes. Cooking time : 30 minutes. Serves 6.

For the samosa covering
½ cup plain flour (maida)
2 teaspoons ghee, melted
salt to taste

For the samosa filling
1 cup boiled potato, cubed
½ cup green peas, boiled
2 tablespoons capsicum, chopped
1 teaspoon cumin seeds (jeera)
¼ teaspoon asafoetida (hing)
2 teaspoons ginger-green chilli paste
2 teaspoons amchur
(dried mango powder)
1 teaspoon coriander-cumin seed
(dhania-jeera) powder
½ teaspoon garam masala
2 tablespoons oil
salt to taste

Other ingredients
oil for deep frying

For the coconut kadhi
1½ cups coconut milk
2 tablespoons Bengal gram flour(besan)
¾ cup fresh curds
2 cardamoms (elaichi)
2 cloves
25 mm. (1") stick cinnamon
1 bay leaf
6 curry leaves
1 teaspoon ginger, grated
1½ teaspoons fresh red chilli, sliced
1 teaspoon oil
salt to taste

For the garnish
½ cup khajur imli ki chutney, page 102
½ cup green chutney, page 105
2 tablespoons chopped coriander
2 tablespoons chopped spring onions
2 to 3 cherry tomatoes, sliced (optional)

For the samosa covering

1. Mix all the ingredients in a bowl and knead into a firm dough using water. Knead well.
2. Divide the dough into 6 equal portions and roll each portion into 125 mm. x 50 mm. (5" x 2") oval (as shown in the diagram below). Keep aside.

For the samosa filling

1. Heat the oil in a pan and add the cumin seeds. When they crackle, add the asafoetida and ginger-green chilli paste.
2. Sauté for 1 minute and add the potato, green peas, capsicum, amchur, coriander-cumin seed powder, garam masala and salt.
3. Mix well and mash lightly.
4. Remove from the fire, cool, divide into 12 equal portions and keep aside.

For the samosas

1. Divide each samosa covering oval into 2 halves.
2. Make a cone from each part and stuff with the filling (as shown in the diagram below).

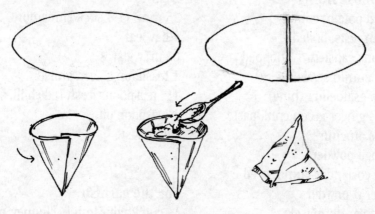

3. Seal the edges carefully using a little water. Repeat with the remaining oval halves and filling to make 11 more samosas.
4. Deep fry in hot oil on a slow flame till golden brown in colour. Keep aside.

For the coconut kadhi

1. Add the gram flour to the curds, mix well and keep aside.
2. Heat the oil in a pan and add the cardamoms, cloves, cinnamon, bay leaf and curry leaves.
3. When the curry leaves splutter, add the ginger and red chilli and stir for a few seconds.
4. Add the coconut milk and 1 cup of water and bring to a boil, while stirring continuously.
5. Add the gram flour-curds mixture and salt and mix well. Simmer on a slow flame till the kadhi thickens while stirring constantly. Keep aside.

How to serve

1. Place the hot samosas in a serving bowl and spoon the hot kadhi over them.
2. Top with the khajur imli ki chutney and green chutney.
3. Garnish with the coriander, spring onions and cherry tomatoes.
   Serve hot.

MINI CHILA CHAAT

Chilas are gram flour pancakes which originated in Rajasthan and which are sold there as roadside snacks. This recipe is of mini gram flour pancakes tossed in a blend of delectable chutneys.

This chaat is delicious when served warm. You can also heat the chilas over a tava (griddle) and let your guests help themselves. Just sprinkle the sev before serving.

Preparation time : 10 minutes.   Cooking time : 15 minutes.   Serves 4.

For the chilas
1 cup Bengal gram flour (besan)
a pinch asafoetida (hing)
1 teaspoon chilli powder
salt to taste
oil for cooking

For the garnish
¼ cup sev, page 113
2 tablespoons chopped coriander

Other ingredients
4 spring onions, finely chopped
½ cup khajur imli ki chutney, page 102
¼ cup green chutney, page 105

For the chilas
1. Mix the gram flour, asafoetida, chilli powder and salt with enough water to make a thin batter.
2. Put about ½ teaspoon of the batter on a non-stick pan and cook with a little oil to make small chilas of about 12 mm. (½") diameter. Cook each chila on both sides until golden brown. The entire batter will make about 80 to 90 chilas.
3. Remove and keep aside.

How to proceed
Just before serving, toss the prepared chilas with the spring onions, khajur imli ki chutney, green chutney and garnish with the sev and coriander.
Serve immediately.

HARIYALI TIKKI AUR CHOLE

Picture on page 103

This potato and methi tikki is filled with cheese. The cheese just melts once the tikkis are fried with the result that the tikkis taste best when they are hot.
Be careful while filling the tikkis with cheese and make sure that the cheese is completely enclosed in the potato covering. Otherwise, the cheese will ooze out of the tikki while it is being fried.
You can enjoy these tikkis with ketchup and can even make a burger out of it.
I love them with hot chole !

Preparation time : 5 minutes. Cooking time : 10 minutes.   Makes 10 tikkis.

1 cup grated boiled potatoes	**For serving**
1 cup chopped fenugreek (methi) leaves	1 recipe chole, page 20
4 green chillies, finely chopped	1 sliced onion
10 cubes mozzarella cheese [cut into 25 mm.(1")cubes]	
salt to taste	
oil for shallow frying	

1. Combine the potatoes, fenugreek leaves, green chillies and salt in a bowl. Mix well.
2. Divide into 10 equal portions and shape each portion into a 50 mm. (2") diameter circle.
3. Place one cube of the cheese in the centre of each circle. Bring the sides together in the centre so as to seal the cheese stuffing inside the potato circle.
4. Roll the tikki between the palms of your hands in such a way that there are no cracks on the surface. Press firmly on top to make flat tikkis.
5. Repeat the procedure and make 9 more tikkis.
6. Shallow fry on both sides in hot oil on a griddle (tava) until golden brown in colour. Serve hot with chole and sliced onion.

Handy tips :
1. *Two medium sized potatoes will give you 1 cup grated potatoes.*
2. *Instead of mozzarella, you can use your favourite cooking cheese.*

TILWALE ALOO KI CHAAT

Baby potatoes coated in a sesame seed paste that is sautéed till it is crisp. This dish has a variety of flavours and textures starting with the humble potato that is coated in a nutty sesame seed paste and then the freshness of mint and coriander contrasting with the sharpness of lemon juice.
This is a chaat to be relished on a rainy day along with a cup of hot tea.

Preparation time : 10 minutes. Cooking time : 25 minutes. Serves 4.

200 grams baby potatoes
5 tablespoons sesame (til) seeds
2 green chillies, chopped
1 onion, chopped
4 tablespoons chopped mint leaves
2 tablespoons chopped coriander
1 teaspoon lemon juice
2 tablespoons oil
salt to taste

1. Boil and peel the potatoes. Keep aside.
2. Grind the sesame seeds to a paste using 2 to 3 tablespoons of water.
3. Heat the oil in a pan, add the green chillies and onion and sauté for 2 to 3 minutes.
4. Add the sesame paste and cook on a slow flame for 4 to 5 minutes till all the water has evaporated.
5. Add the potatoes and salt and sauté for another 2 to 3 minutes.
6. Add the mint, coriander and lemon juice and mix well.
   Serve immediately.

Handy tip : *You can use cubes of boiled potato instead of the baby potatoes.*

You will have heard about the famous Middle Eastern "felafel", but don't you think that the recipe is complicated.

The recipe is inspired by felafel but uses our very own Indian recipe of khulcha stuffed with cheese and broccoli tikkis. Believe me, it's really yummy and yet so simple to make.

Khulcha is a leavened bread which is flavoured with kasuri methi and is either baked, shallow fried or deep fried.

Chole and khulchas are sold in almost every eatery in North India. Khulchas are sold in packets which look similar to those of pizza bases. You only have to reheat them before serving.

You can use your favourite tikkis instead of the cheese and broccoli tikkis and they will taste just as good !

Preparation time : 30 minutes. Cooking time : 30 minutes. Makes 10 pieces.

For the cheese and broccoli tikkis,
Picture on page 51
1 cup finely chopped broccoli
½ cup onion, finely chopped
2 cloves garlic, chopped
2 green chillies, chopped
2 tablespoons cornflour
¾ cup grated cheese
1 cup dried bread crumbs
1 tablespoon oil
salt to taste
oil for shallow frying

For the khulchas
1 cup plain flour (maida)
½ teaspoon fresh yeast, crumbled
½ teaspoon sugar
2 teaspoons dried fenugreek leaves
(kasuri methi)
½ teaspoon crushed pepper
2 teaspoons oil
salt to taste
oil for deep frying

Other ingredients
1 recipe fresh garlic chutney, page 106
1 medium onion, sliced
1 tomato, thinly sliced

For the cheese and broccoli tikkis

1. Heat the oil in a pan and sauté the onion, garlic and green chillies for 2 minutes.
2. Add the broccoli and salt and sauté for 4 to 5 minutes till the broccoli is almost cooked.
3. Remove from the fire, add the cornflour and cheese and mix well.
4. Allow to cool slightly and divide the mixture into 10 equal portions.
5. Roll into the bread crumbs and press firmly on top to make small tikkis.
6. Shallow fry on a tava(griddle) using a little oil till golden brown on both sides.

For the khulchas

1. Combine all the ingredients except the oil in a bowl and knead into a soft dough, using enough water. Knead until it is smooth and elastic (about 5 to 7 minutes).
2. Add the 2 teaspoons of oil and knead well.
3. Cover the dough with a wet muslin cloth and allow it to prove till it doubles in volume (approximately 15 to 20 minutes).
4. Press the dough lightly to remove the air.
5. Divide the dough into 5 equal parts.
6. Roll out each portion into a circle of 125 mm. (5") diameter and 3 mm.(⅛") thickness. Rest for 3 to 4 minutes.
7. Cook the khulchas on a hot tava or griddle on both sides till they are lightly browned. Keep aside.
8. Before serving, deep fry the khulchas in hot oil on both sides till they puff up like puris and are golden brown. Alternatively, shallow fry the khulchas on a hot tava (griddle) using a little oil to cook on both sides. They should puff up.

How to proceed

1. Cut each khulcha into two halves. Each half will have a cavity.
2. Fill every half with a cheese and broccoli tikki. Top with the garlic chutney, sliced onion and tomato.
   Serve hot.

PAKODI CHAAT

We have all eaten dahi pakodis and dahi wadas but can you imagine the same
pakodis in a coconut kadhi? Yes, this is a combination that truly tastes divine.
The fluffy little pakodis which are deep fried and soaked in water go well with a hot
coconut and curd based kadhi topped with a sweet and spicy chutney, lots of sprouts
and spring onions.
The coconut kadhi uses coconut milk which is the liquid extracted with water from the
coconut flesh. Coconut milk is now available in tetrapacks at grocery stores, so you
need not go through the effort of extracting it.

Preparation time : 20 minutes.   Cooking time : 15 minutes.   Serves 4.

For the pakodis	**Other ingredients**
¼ cup urad dal (split black lentils), soaked for 4 hours	1 recipe coconut kadhi, page 57
6 mm. (¼") piece ginger	½ cup khajur imli ki chutney, page 102
1 green chilli, chopped	½ cup green chutney, page 105
a pinch soda bi-carb	¾ cup chopped spring onions
salt to taste	¾ cup moong sprouts, boiled
oil for deep frying	2 tablespoons chopped coriander

For the pakodis
1. Drain the soaked urad dal.
2. Grind together the urad dal, ginger, green chilli and salt in a food processor to a coarse paste, using a little water.
3. Mix the prepared paste with the soda bi-carb adding a little water if required till the batter is light and fluffy.
4. Drop small portions of the batter into hot oil and deep fry on a slow flame till the pakodis are golden brown. (This makes about 24 pakodis)
5. Soak the deep fried pakodis in water for about 45 minutes. Drain.
6. Squeeze out the excess water. Keep aside.

How to proceed
1. Place the pakodis in a serving bowl and pour the hot coconut kadhi over it.
2. Spoon the khajur imli ki chutney and green chutney on top.
3. Top with the spring onions, moong sprouts, coriander and serve immediately.

PYAZ KE SAMOSE

Samosas are probably the most popularly snack eaten in India. Every region has its own recipe using a variety of fillings ranging from the savoury potato vegetable mixture to sweet mava and dry fruit filled samosas.
This recipe is a speciality from the Saurashtra region of Gujarat.
Crispy patti samosas are filled with a fried onion mixture.
Samosa pattis are available at grocery shops and can also be easily made at home.
The art of making samosa lies in folding them into a conical shape in such a way that the filling mixture is completely sealed and it does not burn while deep frying the samosas.
Do not get intimidated by the lengthy making process. These samosas are truly worth the effort.

Preparation time : 20 minutes. Cooking time : 30 minutes. Makes 24 samosas.

For the samosa patti
1 cup plain flour (maida)
1½ tablespoons oil
½ teaspoon salt

Other ingredients
2 tablespoons oil
1 tablespoon plain flour
(maida)

Other ingredients
oil for deep frying

For the filling
4½ cups thinly sliced onions
¼ teaspoon turmeric powder (haldi)
1 teaspoon chilli powder
3 tablespoons coriander-cumin seed
(dhania-jeera) powder
1 teaspoon garam masala
1 tablespoon lemon juice
1½ tablespoons sugar
1 teaspoon cumin seeds (jeera)
½ teaspoon asafoetida (hing)
4 tablespoons Bengal gram flour (besan)
3 tablespoons oil
salt to taste

For the samosa patti
1. Combine the flour, oil and salt in a bowl and knead into a firm dough using approximately ¼ cup of water.

2. Divide the dough into 12 equal portions and roll out each portion into a 50 mm. x 100 mm. (2" x 4") rectangle.
3. On one portion, apply a little oil and sprinkle some flour on top. Place another rolled portion on top and roll both dough rectangles together, sprinkling a little flour to make rolling easier.
4. Repeat the same procedure to make 5 more of these chapatis. Each should be about 100 mm. x 150 mm. (4" x 6").
5. Lightly cook all the chapatis on a tava on both sides and keep aside.
6. When cool, cut each rectangle into 2 lengthwise. Each strip will peel to make 2 thin strips yielding 24 strips in all.

For the filling

1. Lightly salt the sliced onions. Deep fry them in hot oil till they are golden brown and crisp. Be careful not to burn them.
2. Drain on absorbent paper and crush into small pieces.
3. Add the turmeric powder, chilli powder, coriander-cumin seed powder, garam masala, lemon juice, sugar and salt and mix well.
4. In a pan, heat the 3 tablespoons of oil and add the cumin seeds. When they crackle, add the asafoetida.
5. Add the gram flour and roast over a medium flame while stirring continuously. When the gram flour browns lightly, add the fried onion mixture and mix well.
6. Remove from the fire and allow to cool.
7. Divide the filling into 24 equal portions.

How to proceed

1. Fold each samosa patti into a cone (as shown in the diagram below) and stuff with the filling.

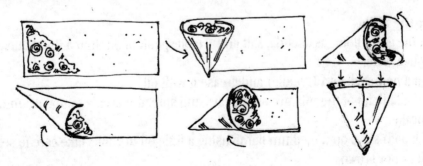

2. Seal the edges using a paste made of plain flour and water.
3. Repeat with the remaining pattis and the filling.
4. Deep fry in oil on a slow flame till golden brown in colour.
   Serve hot with Meethi Soonth, page 107.

STUFFED CHILAS

Picture on page 78

Chilas are pancakes unique to the desert province of Rajasthan. This recipe is of Bengal gram flour chilas stuffed with cubes of paneer, crunchy green peas and tangy tomatoes, tossed together with a dash of chilli and cumin seeds.
At home, we often make besan chilas with onions, tomatoes, coriander and chillies. This recipe however transforms the same old chila into a delightful chaat for your family and friends.

Preparation time : 20 minutes.   Cooking time : 20 minutes.   Serves 4.

For the chilas	For the stuffing
1 cup Bengal gram flour (besan)	2 cups paneer, cubed
a pinch asafoetida (hing)	1 cup green peas, boiled
1 tablespoon oil	½ cup tomatoes, chopped
salt to taste	1 green chilli, chopped
oil for cooking	½ teaspoon cumin seeds (jeera)
	2 tablespoons chopped coriander
	1 teaspoon chaat masala, page 111
Other ingredients	1 tablespoon butter
¼ cup green chutney, page 105	salt to taste

For the chilas

1. Mix the gram flour, asafoetida, salt and 1 tablespoon of oil into a thin batter, using enough water.
2. Heat a non-stick tava (griddle) and grease it with oil.
3. Pour a ladleful of the mixture on the tava and spread it evenly to make a thin pancake.
4. Cook both sides on a medium flame using a little oil to cook. Take care to see that it does not brown.
5. Repeat for the remaining batter to make 12 chilas. Keep aside.

For the stuffing mixture

1. Heat the butter and add the green chilli and cumin seeds.
2. Add the tomatoes and sauté for 2 to 3 minutes.
3. Add the paneer, peas, chaat masala and salt and sauté for a few more minutes.
4. Top with the chopped coriander, divide into 12 portions and keep aside.

How to proceed

1. Place one portion of the stuffing mixture on a chila and fold it to make a semi circle.
2. Top with green chutney and serve hot.

CORN SEV PURI

Picture on page 77

Although every Mumbai visitor never misses eating sev puri, those who have eaten the same thing over the years do grow weary of it.

Here is a recipe for all those who agree with me. Similar but yet very very different from the traditional sev puri.

Baked papadis or little puris are topped with sweet corn and crunchy onions spiked with a tangy ajwain (carom) flavoured tomato chutney. These puris are truly divine and a must try.

All that is required to be kept ready is a batch of baked papadis which can be stored in an air-tight container. You can then easily whip up this recipe at any time of the day when unexpected guests arrive.

Preparation time : 5 minutes.   No cooking.   Serves 4.

To be mixed together into a corn topping	Other ingredients
1 cup yellow corn kernels, boiled	24 baked papadis, page 111
1 cup chopped spring onions	½ cup tamatar ki chutney,
2 green chillies, finely chopped	page 108
1 tomato, finely chopped	1 cup nylon sev or sev, page 113
1 teaspoon chaat masala, page 111	¼ cup fresh pomegranate (anar)
2 teaspoons lemon juice	2 tablespoons chopped
salt to taste	coriander

1. Arrange the papadis on a serving plate.

2. Top each papadi with 1 teaspoon of the corn topping.
3. Put 1 teaspoon of the tamatar ki chutney on each papadi and garnish with the chopped coriander, sev and pomegranate.
   Serve immediately.

ALOO KA BOMB

Our very own version of the "Baked Stuffed Potato", fondly named by street vendors as a "Bomb".
Whole potatoes scooped and stuffed with a chatpata paneer filling and topped with spicy green chutney and crispy sev.

Preparation time : 10 minutes. Cooking time : 15 minutes. Makes 2 bombs.

2 large potatoes, boiled and peeled
1 tablespoon butter

For the paneer filling
½ cup grated paneer
½ teaspoon cumin seeds (jeera)
¼ teaspoon asafoetida (hing)
1 green chilli, chopped
2 tablespoons chopped coriander
2 tablespoons chopped mint
½ teaspoon black salt (sanchal)
1 tablespoon oil
salt to taste

For the topping
sev, page 113
green chutney, page 105

For the paneer filling
1. Heat the oil and add the cumin seeds and asafoetida.
2. When the cumin seeds crackle, add the green chilli, paneer, black salt, salt and mix well.
3. Add the coriander and mint and mix well. Keep aside.

How to proceed
1. Cool the potatoes completely. Cut each into 2 equal parts and scoop out the centres leaving an empty shell.
2. Fill in the paneer mixture and sauté the potatoes in butter till the outside is lightly browned.
3. Place each half on a serving plate and top with the sev and green chutney.
   Serve immediately.

70

Paushtik

CHAAT

MINI DOSA CHAAT

Green gram dosas stuffed with a sweet and spicy pineapple capsicum filling.
I discovered these dosas are so easy to make, as the batter does not require any
fermentation. If you are not the one who can make dosas, just drop spoonfuls of the
batter on a non-stick pan and make great pancakes !
A high protein and carbohydrate packed snack. These dosas are a good beginning to
a meal or those in between times !

Preparation time : 15 minutes. Cooking time : 25 minutes. Makes 20 dosas.

For the dosas	For the stuffing
½ cup split green gram (green moong dal)	1 cup fresh pineapple, chopped
1 green chilli	½ cup capsicum, chopped
½ teaspoon ginger, grated	1 small onion, chopped
a pinch asafoetida (hing)	1 green chilli, finely chopped
1 tablespoon oil	1 teaspoon chilli powder
salt to taste	2 tablespoons butter
oil for cooking	salt to taste

For the dosas
1. Wash and soak the green gram in water for at least 4 hours.
2. Drain and grind to a smooth paste along with the green chilli, ginger and ¼ cup of water.
3. Add the asafoetida, 1 tablespoon of oil, salt and ¼ cup of water and mix well. Keep aside.

For the stuffing
1. Heat the butter and add the onion and green chilli. Sauté for a few minutes till the onion turns translucent.
2. Add the pineapple, capsicum, chilli powder and salt and mix well.
3. Remove from the fire and keep aside.

How to proceed

1. Heat a non-stick tava (griddle) and grease it lightly with oil.
2. When hot, pour a tablespoonful of the dosa batter spread using a circular motion to make a thin dosa approximately 75mm (3")in diameter and cook on one side.
3. Pour a little oil along the edges while cooking.
4. When crispy, place a spoonful of the stuffing on it and roll to form a cylindrical shape.
5. Repeat with the remaining batter and stuffing to make more mini dosas. Serve hot.

FRUIT CHAAT

Picture on page 103

This chaat is sold in the street corners of Delhi. Fruit chaat, as the name suggests, is a blend of assorted fruits (preferably sweet acidic fruits) tossed with potatoes and a delectable blend of chutneys.

Any combination of fruits can be used according to the seasonal availability and personal preferences.

This chaat is packed with nutrients and is also low in calories. This recipe breaks the myth that chaat belongs to the "junk" food category!

Preparation time : 10 minutes.   No cooking.   Serves 4.

For the chaat	For the seasoning
1 cup papaya, diced	1 tablespoon green chutney, page 105
¾ cup pineapple, diced	1 tablespoon khajur imli ki chutney,
1 cup apple, diced	page 102
½ cup banana, diced	¼ teaspoon black salt (sanchal)
4 to 5 gooseberries, cut into	½ teaspoon roasted cumin seed
2 halves each, (optional)	(jeera) powder
¼ cup black and green grapes	1 teaspoon chaat masala, page 111
1 cup cucumber, peeled and diced	¼ teaspoon chilli powder
10 to 12 cherry tomatoes,	juice of ½ lemon
cut into 2 halves	a few springs mint leaves
½ cup boiled potato, diced	salt to taste
½ cup kachalu, boiled and diced (optional)	
2 green chillies, finely chopped	
1 tablespoon chopped coriander	

1. Combine all the chaat ingredients in a bowl and toss well with the seasoning.
2. Serve immediately.

Handy tip : *Chill the fruits thoroughly and add the seasoning just before serving.*

USAL

A traditional Maharashtrian recipe of spicy pulses in a thin watery gravy which is usually eaten with bread.
Usal is served in most streetside eateries in Maharashtra. One such eatery where I never miss the usal is situated on the road from Mumbai to Pune. They serve the most lip smacking usal along with 2 pieces of pav which is filling enough to keep me satiated through the journey.
Another variation that I must mention is Misal. This is nothing but usal topped with fried ganthia and sev. But I prefer the low cal version i.e. without it!

Preparation time : 10 minutes.   Cooking time : 15 minutes.   Serves 4.

1 cup mixed sprouts, page 114
1 teaspoon cumin seeds (jeera)
¼ teaspoon asafoetida (hing)
½ cup chopped onions
1 cup chopped tomatoes
3 to 4 tablespoons dry garlic chutney,
page 106
½ teaspoon turmeric powder (haldi)
2 tablespoons oil
salt to taste

For the garnish
2 tablespoons chopped coriander
¾ cup chopped onions

For serving
4 to 6 lemon wedges
8 laddi pavs (small squares of white bread)

1. Heat the oil in a pan and add the cumin seeds. When they crackle, add the asafoetida.
2. Add the onions and sauté till they are translucent.
3. Add the tomatoes and sauté for another 2 to 3 minutes.
4. Add the garlic chutney and cook till the oil separates.
5. Add the sprouts, turmeric, salt and 2½ cups of water and mix well.
6. Bring to a boil and simmer for 10 to 12 minutes till the sprouts are tender.
7. Top with the coriander and chopped onions.
   Serve with lemon wedges and laddi pav.

VARIATION : MISAL
Top the usal with fried snacks like ganthia and sev and serve immediately.

KHAKRA CHAAT

Picture on facing page

Khakras are extremely popular snacks. They are nothing but thinly rolled out masala (or plain) chapatis with are made crisp over a tava (griddle).

Khakras are readily available at most farsan shops and I get stumped at the variety they come up with each time. The other day, I came across pav bhaji khakras, Punjabi masala khakras, the list was endless! You can however use the flavour you like the most or simply plain khakras.

This recipe uses khakras (broken into pieces) topped with paneer, sweet corn and green peas tossed in an aromatic tomato oregano chutney. This is a recipe that the entire family will relish. It is elegant and truly simple to prepare!

Preparation time : 10 minutes.   Cooking time : 15 minutes.   Serves 4.

12 to 15 khakras, broken into 4 to 6 pieces each
For the tomato chutney
1 onion, chopped
1 teaspoon garlic, grated
4 large tomatoes, blanched, peeled and puréed
¼ cup paneer, cubed
¼ cup sweet corn, boiled
¼ cup green peas, boiled
1 tomato, chopped
1 red chilli, sliced
1 teaspoon sugar
1 teaspoon chilli powder
¼ teaspoon dried oregano
2 tablespoons oil
salt to taste

For the garnish
2 tablespoons chopped coriander

1. **Mini Khasta Kachori,** *page 32*
2. **Potato Basket Chaat,** *page 55*
3. **Corn Sev Puri,** *page 69*
4. **Khakra Chaat,** *recipe above*

For the tomato chutney
1. Heat the oil in a pan, add the onion and garlic and sauté till the onion turns translucent.
2. Add the puréed tomatoes and cook till the oil separates.
3. Add the paneer, sweet corn, green peas, tomato, red chilli, sugar, chilli powder, oregano and salt and sauté for 2 to 3 minutes.
4. Remove from the fire and keep aside.

How to proceed
1. Place the khakra pieces on a serving plate.
2. Top with the tomato chutney and garnish with the chopped coriander. Serve immediately.

Handy tip : *You can even use tortilla chips instead of the khakhras. They taste just as good.*

1. Stuffed Chilas, *page 68*
2. Green Chutney, *page 105*

HARE CHANE KI CHAAT

Another streetside chaat which is so simple to make but yet so delicious. It is a delectable blend of green chana, tomatoes and onions tossed in butter and spiked with a little chaat masala.
Baked papadis added on top lend crunch to this recipe without adding on too many calories.
Stir up this chaat any time in the evening and your family will love it. But remember to make it fresh and serve it hot!

Preparation time : 15 minutes.   Cooking time : 10 minutes.   Serves 4.

2 cups green chana (hara chana), boiled
1 cup onions, finely chopped
3 to 4 green chillies, finely chopped
1 cup tomatoes, finely chopped
1 teaspoon chaat masala, page 111
juice of ½ lemon
2 tablespoons chopped coriander
2 tablespoons butter
salt to taste

For the garnish
8 to 10 baked papadis, crushed, page 111
2 tablespoons sev, page 113

1. Heat the butter in a pan, add the onions and sauté till the onions turn translucent.
2. Add the green chillies, green chana, tomatoes, chaat masala and salt and sauté for a further 2 minutes.
3. Add the lemon juice, coriander and mix well.
4. Serve hot garnished with the crushed papadis and sev.

NON FRIED DAHI VADAS

As they say, necessity is the mother of invention and this recipe came about because I always ended up binging on dahi vadas and the guilt which followed after a deep fried dahi vada snack was immense. But with this recipe, I realised that without compromising on the taste, I could make almost zero fat dahi vadas using a sandwhich toaster.

This recipe however works better using moong dal as compared to urad dal and the addition of a little Eno's fruit salt makes the dahi vadas soft and spongy.

Keep the prepared dahi vadas soaked in water and drain them out just before serving. Top with low fat curds and go ahead, eat as much as you can!

Preparation time : 15 minutes. Cooking time : 15 minutes. Makes 8 vadas.

½ cup split green gram (green moong dal)	**For the tempering**
2 green chillies	½ teaspoon mustard seeds (rai)
a pinch asafoetida (hing)	3 green chillies, broken into pieces
½ teaspoon Eno's fruit salt	a pinch asafoetida (hing)
2 cups fresh curds	1 teaspoon oil
2 pinches roasted cumin seed (jeera) powder	
2 pinches chilli powder	
1 tablespoon chopped coriander (optional)	
salt to taste	

1. Clean, wash and soak the green moong dal for 3 to 4 hours. Drain and keep aside.
2. Add the green chillies and blend in a mixer with very little water.
3. Add the asafoetida and Eno's fruit salt and mix well.
4. Heat a non-stick sandwhich toaster and spread 1 teaspoon of the mixture in each cavity. Close and heat. When ready, the mixture will be toasted into pieces of triangular shape.
5. Remove the toasted pieces and soak them in water for 20 minutes. Thereafter, squeeze out the water and arrange the vadas on a plate.
6. Whisk the curds with the salt.

7. To prepare the tempering, heat the oil and fry the mustard seeds for 1/2 minute. Add the green chillies and asafoetida and pour the seasoning over the whisked curds.
8. Spread the seasoned curds over the vadas. Sprinkle the cumin powder, chilli powder and coriander on top and serve. If you like, also sprinkle khajur imli ki chutney, page 102.

Handy tip: Add the Eno's fruit salt just before you are ready to cook the dahi vadas.

GAJAR AUR MOONG DAL KI CHAAT

Carrots and lentils are tossed with simple spices to make this nutritious chaat which can also be served as a salad.
You can eat large portions of this chaat without the fear of having to exercise for hours to burn out those extra calories!

Preparation time : 15 minutes. Cooking time : 10 minutes. Serves 4.

½ cup yellow moong dal (split yellow gram)
1 cup grated carrots
2 teaspoons chaat masala, page 111
1 tablespoon amchur (dry mango powder)
2 spring onions, chopped
¼ cup chopped raw mango
2 tablespoons chopped mint
2 tablespoons chopped coriander
salt to taste

For the tempering
1 teaspoon mustard seeds (rai)
¼ teaspoon asafoetida (hing)
1 tablespoon oil

1. Clean, wash and parboil the moong dal.
2. Wash in cold water, drain and keep aside.
3. Combine all the ingredients except those for the tempering in a large bowl and mix well.
4. For the tempering, heat the oil in a small pan and add the mustard seeds. When they crackle, add the asafoetida and pour over the prepared chaat.
5. Mix well and serve chilled.

CHaaT
Ke Saath

MELON PANHA

This recipe is an unusual variation to the delicious Mango Panha and tastes just as good.It is an excellant coolant and drives away the heat during the hot summer months!
Melon purée flavoured with cardamom powder is served topped with chilled water.

Preparation time : 10 minutes.   No cooking.   Makes 2 glasses.

2 cups musk melon (kharbuja), diced
4 tablespoons sugar
$\frac{1}{8}$ teaspoon cardamom (elaichi) powder
2 teaspoons lemon juice
ice cubes to serve

1. Combine the musk melon, sugar, cardamom powder and lemon juice and blend into a smooth purée.
2. Pour the melon mixture into 2 serving glasses, top with ice cubes and chilled water. Mix well.
   Serve immediately.
   Handy tip : *You can adjust the sweetness as desired.*

AAM LASSI SLUSH

Mangoes, curds and fresh mint leaves are all the ingredients you require to make this refreshing slush.
Serve it along with a spicy chaat to soothe your taste buds!

Preparation time : 10 minutes.   No cooking.   Serves 4.

2-3 alphonso mangoes, peeled & diced
1½ cups fresh curds
1 tablespoon mint leaves, chopped
4 tablespoons sugar
8 to 10 ice cubes

For the garnish
a few mint leaves

1. Purée all the ingredients in a food processor.
2. Pour the mango curds purée into a shallow freezer proof container. Freeze until slushy for about 4 to 6 hours.
3. Transfer it to a blender and liquidise till it is slushy.
   Serve immediately in small glasses garnished with mint leaves.

KALE ANGOOR KA GOLA

Traditional golas are essentially ice-shavings flavoured with syrup. I have made kale angoor ka gola using fruit purée.
The sweet but acidic pulp of black grapes is balanced by the ripe bananas. Black salt and cumin seed powder add a spike that make this gola so tempting.

Preparation time : 10 minutes.   No Cooking.   Serves 4.

1 cup black grapes
1 banana, finely chopped
2 tablespoons powdered sugar
¼ teaspoon lemon juice
1 teaspoon roasted cumin seed (jeera) powder
¼ teaspoon black salt (sanchal)

1. Blend the black grapes and bananas to a fine purée in a food processor.
2. Add the sugar, cumin seed powder, black salt and ¼ cup of water and mix well.
3. Freeze in a freezer proof container till it has set (approximately 4 to 6 hours).
4. Transfer to a blender and liquidise till it is slushy.
5. Serve scoops of the mixture in 4 glasses .
   Serve immediately.

ADRAK AUR GANNE KA GOLA

The streets of Mumbai are dotted with vendors selling "ganne ka ras" (sugarcane juice) extracted by pressing the sweet " ganna" or sugarcane.
We are so familiar with the sight of fresh sugarcane juice that it is not a novelty. But when the same is frozen with a dash of ginger juice and lemon, it transforms itself into an exciting and delightful sorbet.

Preparation time : 10 minutes.   No cooking.   Serves 4.

6 cups sugarcane juice
1 tablespoon ginger juice
6 to 8 tablespoons sugar
juice of ½ lemon

1. Combine all the ingredients in a bowl and mix well till the sugar dissolves.
2. Freeze in a freezer proof container till it is set (approximately 4 to 6 hours).
3. Transfer to a blender and liquidise till it is slushy.
4. Serve scoops of the gola in 4 glasses and serve immediately.

Handy tip : Grate the ginger to extract ginger juice. Sugarcane juice must be handled and frozen as quickly as possible as the heat and air tend to discolour it and it also turns rancid quickly.

ANAR KA GOLA

The shiny pink seeds of pomegranate are sweet, astringent and acidic. The juice is used in several mocktail recipes!
Here is a recipe of a slush made with fresh pomegranate juice. Chaat masala and black salt add a little tang to the recipe.

Preparation time : 10 minutes.   No cooking.   Serves 4.

6 cups fresh pomegranate seeds, separated
8 tablespoons sugar
¾ teaspoon roasted cumin seed (jeera) powder
½ teaspoon black salt (sanchal)

1. Keep ½ cup of pomegranate seeds aside.
2. Put the remaining pomegranate seeds into a blender and liquidise.
3. Strain the juice and discard the seeds.
4. To the juice, add the sugar, cumin seed powder and black salt and mix well till it dissolves.
5. Freeze in a freezer proof container till it has set (approximately 4 to 6 hours).
6. Transfer to a blender and liquidise till it is slushy.
7. Serve scoops of the mixture in 4 glasses.
   Garnish with the remaining pomegranate seeds and serve immediately.

LEMON GRASS INFUSION DRINK

There is nothing novel about the ingredients used in this drink. It is just a combination of hare chai ki patti, phudina and lemonade which makes a nice cool drink and complements the spicy chaats. I usually lay out a pitcher of this drink when I have parties.

Preparation time : 5 minutes. Cooking time : 10 minutes. Makes 5 glasses.

1 cup lemon grass, finely chopped
1 cup mint leaves, finely chopped
6 tablespoons sugar
juice of 1 lemon
2 bottles of lemonade
ice cubes to serve
mint leaves to garnish
lemon slices to serve

1. Combine the lemon grass, mint leaves and sugar with 2 cups of water in a pan and bring it to a boil.
2. Remove from the fire, allow to cool and purée using a hand blender. Add the lemon juice and mix well. Strain through a muslin cloth to get an infusion.
3. In each serving glass, put 2 to 3 ice-cubes and pour ¼ cup of the infusion.
4. Top with the lemonade and garnish with mint leaves and a lemon slice.
5. Repeat for the remaining infusion and lemonade to make 4 more glasses. Serve immediately.

Handy tip : *Remember to wash the mint and lemon grass thouroughly before using it.*

CHAAT
Ke Baad Kuch Mitha

FRUIT MEIN KULFI

The first time I ever ate this kulfi was at a chaat corner in Delhi. Out of sheer curiosity, I visited this place when I heard of their Stuffed Fruit Kulfi.
What I was served was a frozen mango, which was peeled and sliced. It is then that I realised that the mango had been carefully deseeded and stuffed with kulfi and frozen. So when the fruit was sliced, I could bite into the chilled mango as well as taste a rich, delicious kulfi. It was simply divine!
I tried different versions of this recipe using various fruits but realised that mango and apples complement the kulfi really well. This secret of the stuffed mango, I would like to share with everybody!

Preparation time : 20 minutes.   **Cooking time : 45 minutes.**   **Serves 4.**

2 large mangoes
2 large apples

For the kulfi
1 litre full fat milk
⅓ cup sugar
¼ teaspoon cardamom (elaichi) powder
a few saffron strands
1 tablespoon cornflour

For the kulfi
1. In a small bowl, soak the saffron in a little warm milk and keep aside.
2. Dissolve the cornflour in 2 tablespoons of water and keep aside.
3. Put the milk in a broad non-stick pan and bring it to a boil. Add the cornflour solution and sugar and mix well.
4. Simmer over a medium flame, stirring continuously till the milk reduces to a little less than half the original quantity (approx. 450 ml.).
5. Cool completely, add the cardamom powder and saffron liquid to the mixture and mix well. Keep aside.

How to proceed

1. Slice the top of the mangoes and apples, reserving them for later use.
2. Using a sharp fruit knife, scoop out the mango seeds carefully, taking care not to loosen the pulp inside.
3. For the apples, also scoop out the core and a little of the flesh so that a cavity is created.
4. Fill the cooled kulfi mixture into the scooped fruits and cover with the reserved fruit top. Cover the fruit in a plastic film and freeze for 4 to 6 hours.
5. Just before serving, unwrap the fruits and peel the mangoes.
6. Cut into thick slices horizontally and serve immediately.

GULAB JAMUN

Gulab jamuns are popular all over India. Every region in India serves these khoya rounds deep fried in ghee and soaked in hot saffron flavoured syrup.
The khoya or mava used for the gulab jamuns is of a special kind called Hariali Khoya or Chikna Khoya. It is made by reducing low fat milk and is slightly yellowish in colour and is also loose and sticky in consistency.
Frying these gulab jamuns is an art in itself. The flame has to be sufficiently low so that the gulab jamuns get cooked till the inside.
To finish a round of chaat with these hot jamuns is a most satisfying experience, especially on a cold winter or monsoon evening.

Preparation time : 15 minutes. Cooking time : 45 minutes. Makes 25 jamuns.

For the gulab jamuns
2 cups (250 grams) hariali mava (khoya), grated
5 tablespoons plain flour (maida)
¼ teaspoon cardamom (elaichi) powder

For the sugar syrup
3 cups sugar
a few saffron strands
(optional)

Other ingredients
ghee or vanaspati for deep frying

For the sugar syrup

1. In a large pan, dissolve the sugar in 1½ cups of water and bring to a boil.
2. Simmer over a slow flame till the syrup is of 1 string consistency.
3. Remove any impurities which float on top of the syrup using a slotted spoon.
4. Add the saffron and keep the syrup warm.

For the gulab jamuns

1. In a bowl, combine the khoya, flour and cardamom powder and mix well. Knead to a firm dough without using any water.
2. Divide this mixture into 25 equal portions and roll into rounds. These should have no cracks on the surface as otherwise the gulab jamuns will crack while frying. Refrigerate for 10 to 15 minutes.
3. Deep fry in ghee over a slow flame till the jamuns are golden brown in colour (approximately 10 to 12 minutes).
4. Drain and immerse in the warm sugar syrup. Soak for 30 minutes.
   Serve warm.

MEVA BATI

A richer version of gulab jamuns.
These gulab jamuns are stuffed with chopped dry fruits, saffron and cardamom powder and then deep fried. The khoya or mava used for the gulab jamuns is of a special kind called Hariali Khoya or Chikna Khoya. It is made by reducing low fat milk and is slightly yellowish in colour and is also loose and sticky in consistency. Frying these gulab jamuns is an art in itself. The flame has to be sufficiently low so that the gulab jamuns get cooked till the inside. This a great dessert for a buffet presentation.

Preparation time : 15 minutes. Cooking time : 45 minutes. Makes 24 pieces.

For the gulab jamuns
2 cups (250 grams) hariali mava (khoya), grated
5 tablespoons plain flour (maida)
¼ teaspoon cardamom (elaichi) powder
or whole cardamom seeds

For the filling
¼ cup chopped pistachios
¼ cup chopped almonds
1 tablespoon sugar
a few saffron strands

For the sugar syrup
3 cups sugar
a few strands saffron
(optional)

Other ingredients
¼ teaspoon cardamom
(elaichi) powder
ghee for deep frying

For the sugar syrup
1. In a large pan, dissolve the sugar in 1½ cups of water and bring to a boil.
2. Simmer over a slow flame till the syrup is of 1 string consistency.
3. Remove any impurities which float on top of the syrup by using a slotted spoon.
4. Add the saffron, if desired and keep the syrup warm.

For the gulab jamuns
1. In a bowl, combine all the ingredients, mix well and knead into a firm dough without using any water.
2. Divide the dough into 13 equal portions.
3. Mix one portion of the dough into the ingredients for the filling mixture and divide the filling into 12 equal portions.

How to Proceed

1. Press out each dough portion into a circle of 50 mm. (2") and place one portion of the filling mixture in the centre.
2. Seal the filling mixture in the gulab jamun by bringing the sides together in the centre and roll gently to ensure there are no cracks on the surface.
3. Repeat to make 11 more gulab jamuns.
4. Deep fry in ghee over a slow flame till they are golden brown (approximately 10 to 12 minutes).
5. Drain and transfer into the warm sugar syrup. Soak for at least 30 minutes.
6. Drain, cut each meva bati into 2 equal halves and place on a serving plate.

MALPUAS

Malpuas are rich, soft deep fried pancakes which are soaked in saffron flavoured syrup and eaten warm topped with rabdi or just chopped almonds and pistachios. Traditionally malai malpuas are made from thickened milk or rabdi but this recipe is of instant malpuas using cream.
You will find it easier to cook these malpuas on a non-stick pan, smearing the malpuas with enough ghee whilst cooking.

Preparation time : 5 minutes. Cooking time : 20 minutes. Makes 12 malpuas.

For the malpuas
1 cup (200 grams) cream
4 tablespoons plain flour (maida)
ghee for frying

For the saffron syrup
1 cup sugar
a few saffron strands
2 tablespoons milk
2 teaspoons rose water (optional)

For the garnish
2 tablespoons chopped dry fruits
½ cup instant rabdi, page 116

For the malpuas

1. Mix the cream and flour into a batter.
2. Smear very little ghee on a frying pan and spread a small amount of the batter on it.

3. Fry on both sides using a little ghee until golden brown. Drain on absorbent paper.

For the saffron syrup
1. Dissolve the sugar in 1 cup of water and simmer for 5 minutes to make a syrup of 1 string consistency.
2. Warm the milk in a small bowl, add the saffron and rub until the saffron dissolves. Add to the syrup. Skim off any impurities that float on top using a slotted spoon.
3. Add the rose water and keep the syrup warm.

How to proceed
1. Soak the malpuas in the warm saffron syrup for 2 to 3 minutes and drain.
2. Garnish with dry fruits.
   Serve warm, topped with rabdi.

KESAR KULFI FALOODA

Rich creamy kulfi topped with falooda and rose syurp is a dessert which finds a place at every Indian buffet counter.
Kulfi is our very own Indian ice-cream made from thickened and reduced milk flavoured with saffron and cardamom. Falooda is fresh cornflour "sev" (vermicelli). Kulfi falooda are almost synonymous and make perfect dessert mates. You will find ready dried falooda in the market which has to be rehydrated before use. But of course, nothing is as good as making it yourself!

Preparation time : 10 minutes. Cooking time : 45 minutes.   Serves 5.

For the kesar kulfi	For the falooda sev
1 litre full fat milk	75 grams cornflour
⅓ cup sugar	ice cubes
¼ teaspoon cardamom (elaichi) powder	
a few saffron strands	**For serving**
1 tablespoon arrowroot or cornflour	5 tablespoons rose syrup

For the kesar kulfi

1. In a small bowl, soak the saffron in a little warm milk and keep aside.
2. Dissolve the arrowroot in 2 tablespoons of water and keep aside.
3. Put the milk in a broad non-stick pan and bring it to a boil. Add the arrowroot solution and sugar and mix well.
4. Simmer over a medium flame, stirring continuously till the milk reduces to a little less than half the original quantity (approx. 450 ml.).
5. Cool completely, add the cardamom powder and saffron mixture and mix well.
6. Pour into 5 kulfi moulds and freeze overnight till it sets.

For falooda sev

1. Mix the cornflour very well in 450 ml. of water to make a smooth solution.
2. Put the mixture to boil on a slow flame. Go on stirring and cooking until the mixture becomes translucent.
3. Put the mixture in a "sev" press and squeeze by hand through the sieve into a vessel which is filled with chilled water and with ice cubes. This falooda "sev" must be preserved in water till required.

How to proceed

1. To unmould the kulfi, allow the kulfi moulds to remain outside the refrigerator for 5 minutes and then unmould by inserting a wooden skewer stick or a fork, in the centre of the kulfi and pulling it out.
2. Put 3 teaspoons of rose syrup and 1 tablespoon of falooda "sev" in each serving bowl. Top with cubes of kesar kulfi.
   Serve immediately.

INSTANT JALEBIS

Fresh hot syrupy jalebis are a hit at any chaat party. You will always find serpentine queues of people waiting to savour this delicacy.
You will not believe how quickly jalebis can be made. I have used yeast to ferment the jalebi batter quickly and so it does not require to be left for a day to ferment. The trick here is to immediately start frying the jalebis once the batter has rested for 10 minutes. If the batter is left for a longer period, it ferments and the jalebis lose shape. Also remember to soak the jalebis in warm sugar syrup immediately after frying them. Yes, they are made as simply as that!

Cooking time : 15 minutes. Preparation time : 10 minutes. Makes 15 jalebis.

For the jalebi batter
1 cup plain flour (maida)
1 teaspoon Bengal gram flour (besan)
½ teaspoon fresh yeast, crumbled
1 tablespoon melted ghee
1 teaspoon sugar
2 to 3 drops of lemon yellow food colouring

For the sugar syrup
2 cups sugar
a few saffron strands
¼ teaspoon lemon juice

Other ingredients
ghee for deep frying

For the jalebi batter
1. Sieve the plain flour and gram flour together.
2. Dissolve the yeast in 1 tablespoon of water.
3. Mix the flour mixture, yeast solution, ghee, sugar and lemon yellow food colouring with ⅔ cup of water to make a thick batter, making sure that no lumps remain.
4. Keep aside for 10 minutes till the yeast ferments.

For the sugar syrup
1. Dissolve the sugar in 1 cup of water and simmer for 5 minutes till the syrup is of 1 string consistency.
2. Add the saffron and lemon juice and mix.
3. Remove from the fire and keep aside.

How to proceed
1. Heat the ghee in a broad saucepan [the ghee should be approximately 25 mm. (1") deep].
2. Fill the jalebi batter into a piping bag with a single hole nozzle or a thick cloth with a small hole in the centre which is finished with button-hole stitch.
3. Press out round whirls of the batter into the hot ghee working closely from centre to the outside of the whirl [approximately 50 mm. (2") diameter].
4. Deep fry the jalebis till golden brown and transfer into the warm sugar syrup.
5. Drain immediately and serve hot.

Handy tips :
1. *Do not allow the jalebi batter to overferment.*
2. *Fry the jalebis immediately once the batter has rested for 10 minutes.*

MEVA MOODI

Crunchy salted dry fruits and puffed rice coated with melted jaggery tossed in pure desi ghee. Crisp and chewy, this is best savoured with your fingers while it is still warm.

This snack derives its origin from the streets of Calcutta. Meethi moodi essentially means sweetened puffed rice or mamra.

A special kind of jaggery called Nalini Gur is used for it but honey and ordinary jaggery when used together are comparable to this. Use ready salted dry fruits for this recipe. It might be a good idea to toast the nuts and the puffed rice in a slow oven for a few minutes before adding them to the moodi.

Assemble this recipe just before serving.

Preparation time : 5 minutes.   Cooking time : 5 minutes.   Serves 4.

1 cup puffed rice (mamra)
¼ cup toasted salted almonds
¼ cup toasted salted pistachios
¼ cup toasted salted cashewnuts
¼ cup salted peanuts
¼ cup jaggery (gur), grated
2 teaspoons honey
1 teaspoon ghee

1. Heat the ghee in a non-stick pan, add the jaggery and honey and cook on a very slow flame till the jaggery has just melted (approx. 2 to 3 minutes).
2. Add the remaining ingredients and toss lightly.
   Serve hot.

Handy tips :

1. Do not overheat the jaggery since the moodi will have a bitter aftertaste if it caramelises.

2. Add a teaspoon of water to the jaggery to prevent it from burning quickly.

3. Do not multiply this recipe while cooking. It is always better to prepare it in small batches.

Chatpati Chutney

CHAat

KHAJUR IMLI KI CHUTNEY

*This sweet and sour chutney blend spruces up almost all chaat recipes.
The addition of jaggery makes the chutney sweeter, but you may omit it if you prefer a
more tangy flavour.
An essential accompaniment to most chaats, this chutney can be stored refrigerated
for upto a month and deep frozen for more than 6 months.*

Preparation time : 10 minutes.   Cooking time : 15 minutes. Makes 2 cups.

2 cups dates (khajur), deseeded
¼ cup tamarind (imli), deseeded
1 cup jaggery (gur), grated
1 teaspoon chilli powder
a pinch asafoetida (hing)
salt to taste

1. Wash the dates and tamarind and place them in a saucepan.
2. Add the jaggery, chilli powder, asafoetida, salt and 4 cups of water and simmer
   for 20 to 25 minutes.
3. Cool and strain the mixture through a sieve.
   Use as required. Store refrigerated.

Handy tip : *You can also purée the chutney in a food processor and then
strain it.*

1. **Fruit Chaat,** *page 74*
2. **Chole,** *page 20*
3. **Hariyali Tikki,** *page 61*

GREEN CHUTNEY

Picture on page 78

*A green mint and coriander flavoured chutney which is great for sandwich spreads.
Mint adds freshness to this chutney. The addition of lemon juice enhances the
flavours of mint and coriander and prevent discoloration of the greens.
Green chutney is probably the most favourite Indian accompaniment.
Crispy samosas, dhoklas etc. are considered incomplete without this chutney.
The chutney can be stored refrigerated for upto a week.*

Preparation time : 10 minutes.   No cooking.   Makes 1 cup.

2 cups chopped mint leaves
1 cup chopped coriander
1 large onion, sliced
juice of 1 to 2 lemons
1 tablespoon sugar
4 to 6 green chillies
salt to taste

1. Combine all the ingredients and grind to a smooth paste in a blender using very
   little water.
2. Refrigerate and use as required.

1. **Tamatar ki Chutney,** *page 108*
2. **Samosa Kadhi Chaat,** *page 57*

FRESH GARLIC CHUTNEY

Picture on page 51

A must have ingredient in any chaat. The pungent aroma of garlic is unmistakable. Oil your hands before you peel garlic to prevent your fingers from discolouring and to prevent having a lingering garlic aroma throughout the day! Soaking garlic cloves in hot water makes it easier to peel them. Make this chutney in large quantities. It stays well refrigerated for upto two weeks.

Preparation time : 5 minutes.   No cooking.   Makes ¾ cup.

1 cup garlic cloves, peeled
1 tablespoon chilli powder
juice of ½ lemon
salt to taste

1. Combine all the ingredients in a blender with ¼ cup of water and grind to a fine paste.
2. Before using, dilute with water and use as required.

DRY GARLIC CHUTNEY

A traditional Maharashtrian recipe. Dry coconut imparts a nutty and oily taste to the chutney. This chutney is also popularly known as vada pav chutney.

Preparation time : 5 minutes. Cooking time : 2 minutes.   Makes ½ cup.

⅓ cup garlic cloves, peeled
¼ cup dried coconut (kopra), grated
2 tablespoons chilli powder
1 teaspoon oil
salt to taste

1. Heat the oil in a pan and sauté the garlic and coconut for 2 to 3 minutes over a medium flame.
2. Cool, combine all the ingredients in a blender and grind till it is a smooth mixture. Use as required.

MEETHI SOONTH

A sweet and tangy Marwari chutney made of dried mango slices with a predominant flavour of dried ginger powder (soonth). This is also called Navratna Chutney.

Preparation time : 10 minutes. Cooking time : 25 minutes. Makes 1½ cups.

12 dried mango slices
½ cup grated jaggery (gur)
½ cup sugar
¼ cup dried dates (kharek)
¼ cup broken cashewnuts
2 tablespoons sultanas
1 teaspoon chilli powder
½ teaspoon dried ginger powder (soonth)
1 teaspoon fennel seeds (saunf)
½ teaspoon roasted cumin seeds (jeera)
salt to taste

1. Soak the dates and cashewnuts in warm water.
2. In a pan, combine the mango slices, jaggery and sugar with 1 cup of water and simmer for 20 minutes till the mango slices are soft.
3. Cool completely and purée into a fine paste.
4. Drain the soaked dates and cashewnuts. Deseed and chop the dried dates.
5. Add all the ingredients into the puréed chutney mixture and mix well.
   Use as required. Store refrigerated.

Handy tip : *Dried mango slices are available at most grocers. You can substitute the slices with approximately 2-3 tablespoons amchur powder.*

TAMATAR KI CHUTNEY

Picture on page 104

*Ajwain and garlic flavoured tomato chutney. Freeze large quantities of this chutney,
scoop out small portions of it and reheat for use.*

Preparation time : 10 minutes. Cooking time : 20 minutes. Makes 1 cup.

8 medium sized tomatoes
1 teaspoon ajwain (carom seeds)
a pinch asafoetida (hing)
1 tablespoon garlic, grated
1 teaspoon chilli powder
1 teaspoon sugar
2 tablespoons oil
salt to taste

1. Blanch the tomatoes in hot water. Peel and purée in a liquidizer.
2. Heat the oil in a pan, add the ajwain and asafoetida and sauté for 30 seconds.
3. Add the garlic and sauté for a few seconds.
4. Add the puréed tomatoes, chilli powder, sugar and salt and bring to a boil.
5. Simmer for 20 minutes or till the oil has separated. Cool and use as required.

Basic Recipes

CHAAT

PAPADI

Crispy small flat puris. They can be plain or spiced up.
They add crunch to most chaat recipes. Remember to make the papadi dough stiff
and to roll it out as thinly as possible. Prick each papadi well before frying to ensure
that it does not puff up.
You can choose to roll out small puris or a large dough circle and cut out small
rounds using a cookie cutter.
You can use either plain flour or whole wheat flour or a combination of the two.
Make large quantities of this recipe, so that you can rustle up a recipe when
unexpected guests arrive!

Preparation time : 10 minutes. Cooking time : 10 minutes. Makes 80 papadis.

2 cups plain flour (maida)
2 level teaspoons ajwain (carom seeds)
1 tablespoon oil
salt to taste
oil for deep frying

1. Mix the flour, ajwain, oil and salt and add enough water to make a firm dough.
2. Knead well and roll out into small thin rounds of about 40 mm. (1½") diameter, without using flour if possible. Prick with a fork.
3. Deep fry in hot oil over a medium flame until golden brown and crisp.
4. Cool and store in an air-tight container.
   Use as required.

CHAAT MASALA

Picture on page 25

One flavour that most snacks rely on for their zip is chaat masala.
Chaat masala is a spice blend consisting of black salt, chilli powder, cumin seeds and
dry mango powder.
There are as many recipes for chaat masalas as there are households in India,
but this one is a personal favourite!
Store this masala in an air-tight container.

Preparation time : a few minutes.   No cooking.   Makes 4 cups.

1 cup slightly roasted coriander seeds (dhania)
1 cup Kashmiri red chillies, roasted
1 cup roasted cumin seeds (jeera)
1 cup amchur (dry mango powder)
3 tablespoons black pepper corns
1 cup salt
3 tablespoons black salt (sanchal)

1. Powder all the ingredients together in a grinder.
2. Store in an air-tight container.
   Use as required.

BAKED PAPADIS

This is a virtually fat free recipe for all low cal food lovers!
Crispy baked puris are delicious at any time of the day.
You can spice up the dough, if you prefer, adding a little chilli powder and cumin
seeds. I personally like them just plain. Again, I would suggest that you store large
quantities in an air-tight container.

Preparation time : 5 minutes. Cooking time : 10 minutes. Makes 40 puris.

1 cup (125 grams) whole wheat flour (gehun ka atta)
1 teaspoon oil
¼ teaspoon salt

1. Mix the flour, oil and salt. Add water and prepare a stiff dough. Knead well.
2. Divide the dough into 40 portions.
3. Roll out into thin puris and prick with a fork.
4. Arrange the puris on a lightly greased baking tray.
5. Bake in a hot oven at 200°C (400°F) for 10 minutes.

Handy tip : *This wholesome substitute for the traditional fried and greasy puris uses the superior fat reducing method of baking.*

CURDS

Curds or "dahi" is an item that Indian households consume at all times of the day. But what is essential to make a good chaat are good fresh curds. For those who love thick curds, use full fat milk, along with a tablespoon of milk powder dissolved in milk and needless to say, use skimmed milk for low calorie curds.

Preparation time : 5 min.   Setting time : 6 hours.   Makes 5 cups.

1 litre full fat milk
1 tablespoon curds (made the previous day)

1. Warm the milk.
2. Add the curds, mix well and cover.
3. Keep aside until the curds set (approximately 5 to 6 hours). During the cold climate, place inside a cupboard or closed oven to set.
4. Refrigerate after the curds have set and use as required.

SEV

*This crisp vermicelli made of gram flour is used to top almost all chaats.
Mounds of different types of sevs are displayed at almost all farsan shops. The variety
of flavours you get includes palak sev, garlic sev, pepper sev etc. Just name it and it is
available!
But did you know that making sev at home was as simple as this!*

Preparation time : 5 minutes. Cooking time : 15 minutes.   Makes 2 cups.

1 cup Bengal gram flour (besan)
2 tablespoons hot oil
¼ teaspoon asafoetida (hing)
¼ teaspoon turmeric powder (haldi)
salt to taste

oil for deep frying

1. Combine the Bengal gram flour, oil, asafoetida, turmeric powder, salt and approximately 3 tablespoons of water to make a stiff dough.
2. Fill the dough into a sev "press" and press out thin strands into hot oil. Deep fry on a slow flame till light brown and crisp.
3. Cool and store in an air-tight container.

Handy tip : *You can also flavour the batter with chilli powder or garlic paste or spinach purée to make spicy sev, garlic sev or spinach sev.*

MIXED SPROUTS

Picture on page 26

Ready sprouts are available at most grocery stores. But did you know that making sprouted beans was as easy as this.

Preparation time : 2 days   No cooking.   Makes 3 cups.

1 cup mixed beans
(whole moong, chick peas, green chana, brown chana, matki etc.)

1. Wash the beans and soak in water for a minimum of 4 hours.
2. Drain and wash thoroughly.
3. Keep in a jar covered with a piece of cloth for 5 to 6 hours.
4. Place in the refrigerator overnight.
5. Next day, wash thoroughly, drain and again keep in a jar covered with a piece of cloth for 5 to 6 hours. They will have started germinating by now.
6. Place in the refrigerator overnight.
7. Sprinkle water on the sprouted beans on the third day and store in the refrigerator until required for use.

Handy tips :
1. *In the process of sprouting, Vitamins A, B group and C (which are otherwise absent in ordinary beans) are formed.*
2. *Beans are very rich in proteins, complex carbohydrates and iron.*

BOONDI

Picture on page 26

Crispy fried gram flour drops, they resemble little yellow pearls!
Semolina crispens the boondi. Large quantities of boondi can be fried and stored in air-tight containers.
You can garnish curds with crispy boondi or soak the boondi in water for some time before using.

Preparation time : 10 minutes. Cooking time : 30 minutes. Makes 2½ cups.

1 cup Bengal gram flour (besan)
2 teaspoons semolina (rava)
1 teaspoon salt
oil for deep frying

1. Combine the gram flour, semolina and salt with approximately ¾ cup of water and prepare a smooth batter.
2. Heat the oil in a kadhai and pour 3 to 4 tablespoons of the batter at a time over a boondi jhara (large perforated spoon) so that boondi drops into the hot oil (Hold the spoon 3 to 4 inches above the height of the oil).
3. Fry the boondi over a medium flame. Remove using a slotted spoon and drain on absorbent paper. Store in an air-tight container.
   Use as required.

INSTANT RABDI

This is an instant recipe that uses bread to thicken the rabdi almost instantly. It reduces the time and energy we spend labouriously stirring the milk till it thickens, it is also lower in fat content.

Preparation time : 10 minutes. Cooking time : 15 minutes. Serves 4.

2 cups milk
2 bread slices
¼ cup condensed milk
2 tablespoons sugar
¼ teaspoons cardamom (elaichi) powder
a few saffron strands

1. Remove the crusts of the bread slices and discard. Grind the bread slices in a food processor to make fresh bread crumbs. Keep aside.
2. Bring the milk to boil in a heavy bottomed pan. Add the fresh bread crumbs, condensed milk and sugar and cook on a high flame, while stirring continuously (approx.10 minutes).
3. Remove from the fire, add the cardamom powder and saffron and mix well.
4. Refrigerate for 2 to 3 hours and serve chilled.